Leicestershire & Rutland

Roger Noyce

COUNTRYSIDE BOOKS
NEWBURY BERKSHIRE

First published 2010
© Roger Noyce 2010

COUNTRYSIDE BOOKS
3 Catherine Road
Newbury, Berkshire

To view our complete range of books,
please visit us at
www.countrysidebooks.co.uk

ISBN 978 1 84674 176 0

Cover picture of Foxton Locks
by David Hunter
(Pictures of Britain)

Designed by Peter Davies, Nautilus Design

Produced through MRM Associates Ltd., Reading
Typeset by CJWT Solutions, St Helens
Printed in Thailand

Contents

AREA MAP SHOWING LOCATIONS OF THE WALKS

Contents

PUBLISHER'S NOTE

Introduction

Leicestershire and Rutland is a superb area of beautiful scenery and traditional English pubs, comparing well with the Chilterns, the Cotswolds and the West Country. After reading this book and walking the routes, you too will be amazed at the diversity of the landscape. This is a secret countryside with the city of Leicester at its very centre.

Ever since the Romans established Ratae (Leicester), the county has had historical associations. The city of Leicester is the largest in the East Midlands, being the traditional county town of Leicestershire. The adjoining county of Rutland, with Oakham as its capital, is the smallest normal unitary authority (in terms of population) in mainland England; only the City of London is smaller.

The choice of walks for this book has caused me much heart-searching because the area holds so many attractive routes with very many places of interest to visit. I have tended towards walks with exceptional scenery and, inevitably, there is always a good pub in the area. From the rolling hills in the east and the National Forest area to the beautiful Belvoir Castle – what a selection of brilliant places to visit! Often, there is an abundance of riches in just one village.

Charnwood Forest is now part of the new National Forest that is being created for the nation across 200 square miles of the East Midlands, embracing parts of Leicestershire, Staffordshire and Derbyshire. In just over ten years, more than seven million trees have been planted. Charnwood Forest covers some 6,100 acres in north-western Leicestershire, bounded by Leicester, Loughborough and Coalville. It is undulating and rises to over 600 ft, rocky and picturesque, with barren areas, and some extensive tracts of woodland. It has become an important recreational area with forest trails, noted for their displays of bluebells in the early spring, rock climbing and hill walking.

The walks vary in length between 1¾ miles and 6 miles, and offer a variety of scenery from the Vale of Belvoir in the north of Leicestershire to the River Soar flood-plain near Leicester; from the stunning beauty of Rutland Water to the superb lakes at Staunton Harold near the famous Calke Castle. One of the walks embraces Bosworth Field where the famous battle was fought at the end of the Wars of the Roses on 22nd August 1485. Another of the routes takes you through Bradgate Park and passes the Old John, a folly sited at the very top of the highest hill in the park and well known for its 'mug-shape', the 'handle' of which was added later, apparently in memory of a beer-loving family retainer.

Several walks are in the tiny but beautiful county of Rutland. Rutland Water, built in the 1970s to supply water to the East Midlands, covers

3,100 acres and has a 25-mile shoreline. It has become Rutland's most popular tourist attraction, offering activities for all ages. And after your walk around Rutland Water you can visit the Egleton and Lyndon nature reserves, or just relax by the water and watch the action from the shoreline. One of Rutland's most famous landmarks is Normanton church, a beautiful old building that was saved from the water and now houses an exhibition about the building of the reservoir, containing fossils and an Anglo-Saxon skeleton.

Directions are given for places to park your car while you walk, and at all the walk locations you will find attractive pubs offering fine English beer, or another source of refreshments. The length of the walks should suit all the family and most can be completed in either a morning or afternoon session allowing you the opportunity to visit places of interest nearby.

Depending upon the season in which you walk you will find variations in the terrain, but always be prepared for muddy patches in parts as this is an area of heavy clay, at least in the west, often near water meadows, along bridleways or across fields. Occasionally, you may have to walk over a ploughed field if that is the right of way, unless you can get around the edge successfully. Even the most accommodating of pub landlords is unlikely to welcome walkers with muddy boots and wellingtons, so please show appropriate respect.

Do observe the Countryside Code at all times and treat the landscape with respect. Also be aware that the countryside is constantly changing so paths can get diverted or stiles replaced with gates, for instance. However, you should still be able to complete the routes by following the directions in the book. So put on your boots and get out and stroll in the marvellous counties of Leicestershire and Rutland.

Roger Noyce

ACKNOWLEDGEMENT

I gratefully acknowledge the help that I have received from my wife Margaret and her photographs fill this book.

1 Barkestone-le-Vale and Belvoir Castle

The old Grantham Canal

The Walk 3½ miles   Allow 2 hours
Map OS Explorer 260 Nottingham (GR 778349)

How to get there

Barkestone-le-Vale is in the north-east of the county, some 10 miles north of Melton Mowbray and north-west of Belvoir Castle. It can be accessed from the A607 or the A52. **Parking:** On the road near the church.

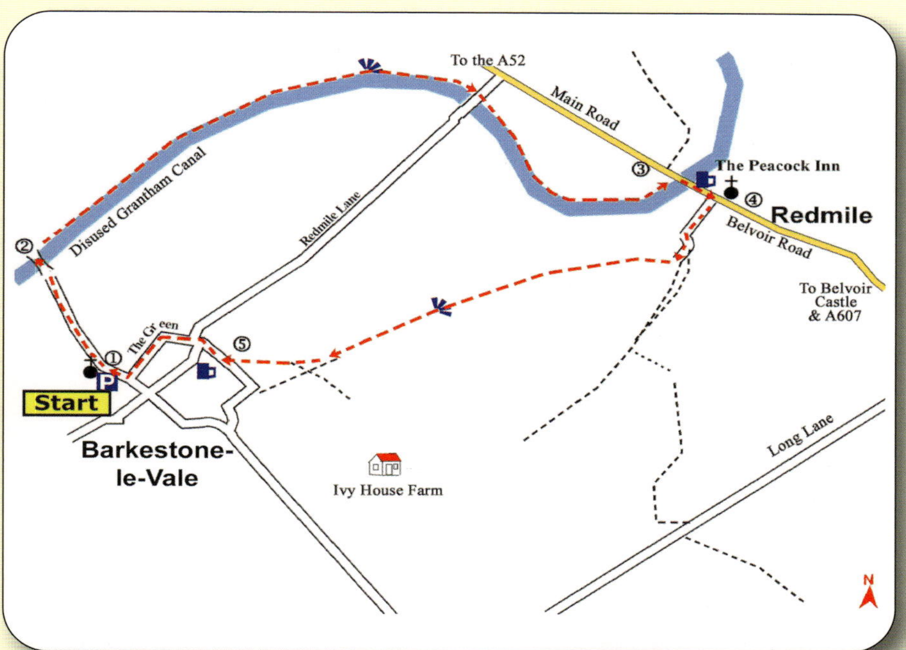

Introduction

This pleasing stroll takes you along the towpath of the disused Grantham Canal where you should see an abundance of wild flowers depending on the time of year. Swans also frequent the water here. There are superb views of Belvoir Castle to enjoy, before reaching the lovely village of Redmile which is a tiny village on the border with Nottinghamshire and sited near to the canal. The return route takes you over undulating land back into Barkestone-le-Vale.

Refreshments

The **Peacock Inn** in nearby Redmile, passed at point 3 of the walk is one of two fine pubs in this pretty Leicestershire village. The oldest part was built in 1704 and it once belonged to the Duke of Rutland. It is a traditional country pub, with beamed ceilings and open fires in the colder months. There is an extensive bar menu and à la carte dining in the restaurant. At weekends, breakfasts are also on offer from 8.30 am to 10.30 am. Telephone: 01949 842554; www.thepeacockinnredmile.co.uk

THE WALK

①

From your parked car outside the church, walk down the lane until you reach the bridge over the disused **Grantham Canal**.

 **②**

Turn left and descend to the towpath of the old canal. Turn left under the bridge then continue along the towpath – in midsummer you can expect the canal to be lined with meadowsweet and bull-rushes. Proceed along the towpath for some 1¼ miles. Walk under the footbridge near to the sewage works and pass over a road-bridge as the route bends right. Soon the towpath bends left and you will have a superb view of the old canal with **Belvoir Castle** on the hill ahead.

Belvoir is a truly magnificent castle offering a commanding position across the Vale of Belvoir; the present castle is the fourth to have stood on the site since Norman times. It was completed in the early 19th century after previous buildings suffered complete or partial destruction. The turrets of the castle towers can be seen peering over the trees from several positions on the walk. For opening times and admittance prices, telephone 01476 871002; www.belvoircastle.com

Swans among the reeds

On the way back to Barkestone-le-Vale

Leave the towpath and ascend to the road pavement on the edge of the lovely village of **Redmile**. As you stroll down the main street you will pass by (or visit, perhaps) the **Peacock Inn** and see the beautiful old **church of St Peter** on your left.

The turret clock of St Peter's church strikes the hour on the tenor bell. It is still hand wound and due to the insertion of a new ceiling the weights are unable to travel the original distance and the clock now needs winding every five days. The single dial on the south face of the tower is of cast-iron and painted blue with gold numerals. It was last painted for the Queen's Silver Jubilee in 1977.

Turn down **Church Lane** on the right and continue into the residential road. At its end bear right onto a clear waymarked footpath and follow the signs. These will take you through a metal gate and onto open land. After bearing left through another gate, follow the clear footpath as it ascends pastureland to a stile at the top of the rise. Go over this and continue up the hill, pausing from time to time to see the fine retrospective view that eventually embraces **Belvoir Castle**. Continue up the field and eventually you will reach a stile onto the road in **Barkestone-le-Vale**.

Turn right and stroll to the end of the road to reach the main road. Now go left along the lane called **The Green** and turn right into **Jericho Lane** to find the **church of St Peter and St Paul** to your right.

The church of St Peter and St Paul dominates the landscape. There must have been a church here for some thousand years but the present building dates back to 1639, when mention was made of its bells. The church was restored in 1840.

PLACE OF INTEREST NEARBY

Belvoir Castle is just two-thirds of a mile to the east of Barkestone. A visit to this magnificent place with its stunning state rooms and wonderful gardens is a must. For opening times, telephone: 01476 871002; www.belvoircastle.com

2 Castle Donington and Daleacre Hill

Lockington village seen from across the fields

The Walk 3¾ miles Allow 3 hours
Map OS Explorer 245 The National Forest (GR 452276)

How to get there

Castle Donington is in the north-west of the county, just 2 miles west from junction 24 of the M1. It can be accessed from the A6 or the A453. **Parking:** With consideration by the metal fence of Castle Donington cemetery.

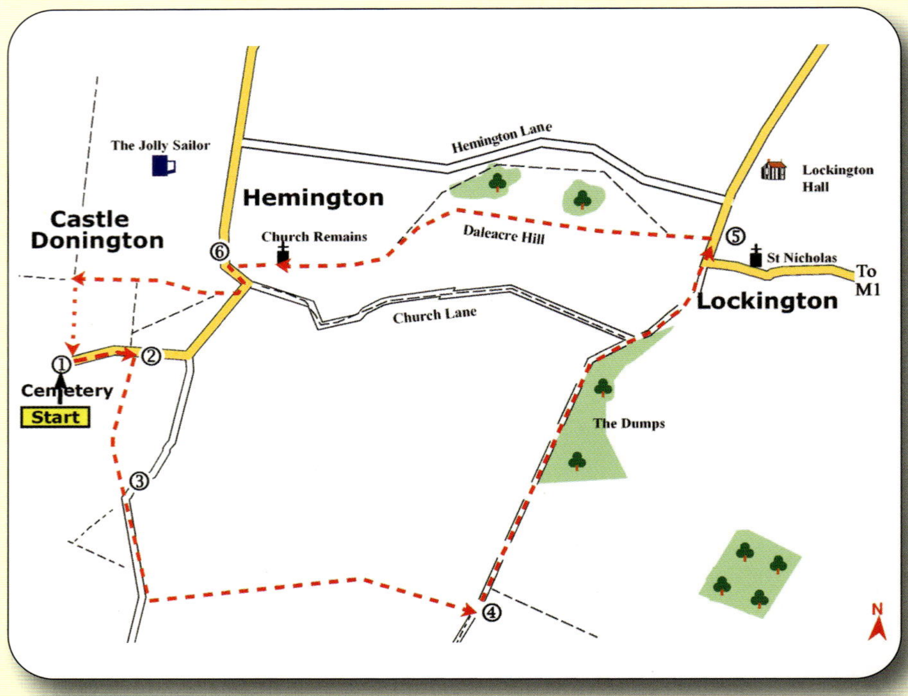

Introduction

This is a short but very pleasing walk into the village of Lockington, with a superb ascent over the lovely Daleacre Hill, from where you will have good views of the surrounding countryside. The return route is through Hemington, another interesting village.

Refreshments

The **Jolly Sailor** at Hemington is a traditional pub serving real ales and good food. Telephone: 01332 810448.

THE WALK

Castle Donington is a large village almost considered a town, with a population of around 7,000. It is the closest village to East Midlands Airport and is also home to the world-famous Donington Park motor racing circuit. The village itself is a *mix of the old and new, with modern shops alongside dignified Georgian and Regency houses. Several timber-framed houses dating from the 17th century and earlier survive along the main road of the village.*

From the parking area outside the cemetery fencing on the edge of **Castle Donington**, descend the road that goes towards the village of **Hemington**.

In about 100 yards, turn right and go over the stile to stroll along the hedged footpath, going generally southwards. In about 150 yards you will arrive in a farm field and diagonally cross the field to reach a lane.

Turn right and ascend the lane for about 50 yards, then turn left onto a firm footpath going generally eastwards. The path tends to hug the field hedge, going through a field hedge gap and then passing through another gap for you to walk around the left field edge to reach a good track.

Turn left along this track and descend by the side of woodland called the **Dumps**. After descending the track you will pass **Church Lane** (to the left) and then begin to ascend, bending right and then left to arrive in the village of **Lockington**. Walk up **Main Street** and you will pass the lane to **St Nicholas' church** (on the right).

One of the firm paths along the way

The church of St Nicholas in Lockington is an early Gothic building and there are a number of 13th-century thatched cottages in this small village.

  ⑤

Turn left into **Kingsgate** and proceed up the hedged footpath at the rear of houses. You will soon pass through a hand gate and begin the delightful ascent of **Daleacre Hill**. In the days when we had snow, this hill was once popular for sledging. Descend the far side and proceed through stiles and hand gates as you approach the village of **Hemington**. Pass the remains of an old church and arrive in the village near to the war memorial.

  ⑥

Turn left and ascend the tarmac footpath opposite. This footpath leads you above the village. At the top take the right-hand footpath that soon descends the other side of the hill. Follow the clear waymarked footpath going generally westwards. Continue along this clear footpath until you reach a junction of footpaths where you turn left and ascend the slope to the road. Your car will be to the right opposite.

The ruined church at Hemington

PLACE OF INTEREST NEARBY

Castle Donington Race Track is the home of the British Motorcycle Grand Prix. In 2010 British Grand Prix F1 returns to Donington Park after a 17-year absence when it last hosted the Grand Prix of Europe in 1993. You can visit the Donington Grand Prix Exhibition, the largest collection of Grand Prix racing cars in the world. Information is available from www.donington-park.co.uk.

3 Buckminster and Sproxton

Buckminster church

The Walk 6 miles 🕐 Allow 3½ to 4 hours
Map OS Explorer 247 Grantham (GR 879230)

How to get there

Buckminster is on the B676, east of Melton Mowbray, and just west of Colsterworth on the A1. **Parking:** Near the church of St John the Baptist, Buckminster.

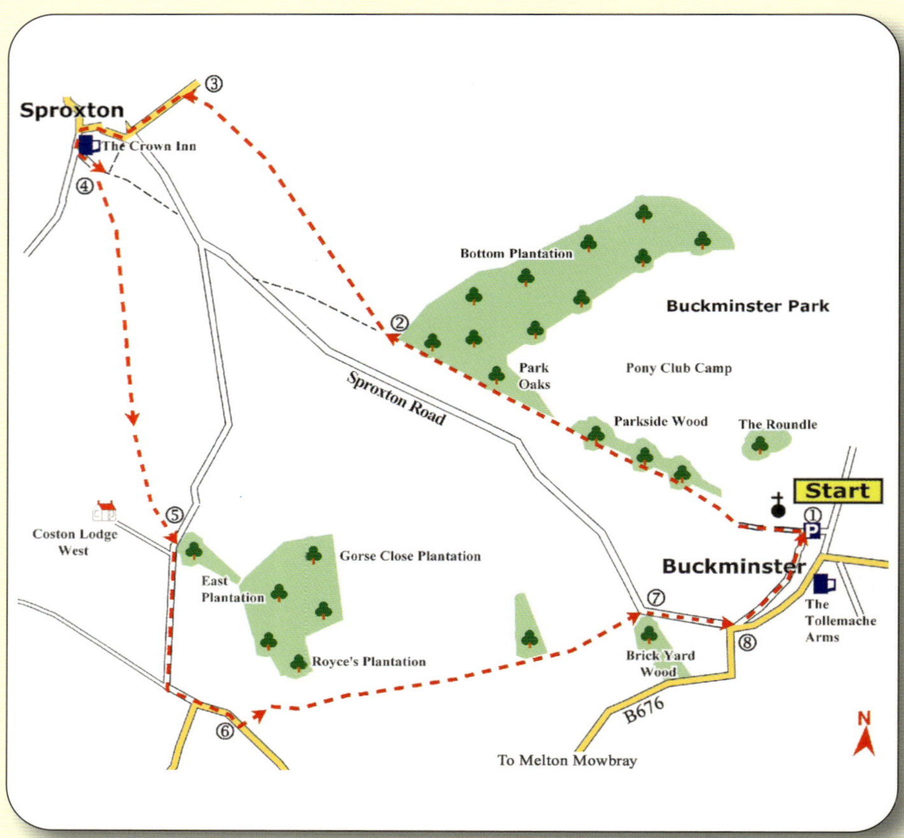

Introduction

This is a splendid stroll into the beautiful countryside of north Leicestershire, following, for a short time, the Mowbray Way, a path of just under 9 miles that links Scalford in the west with Buckminster, before arriving in the pretty village of Sproxton.

Refreshments

The **Crown Inn** at Sproxton, a stone-built freehouse in the village, is a traditional English pub in the heart of the Leicestershire countryside that has been welcoming customers for over 140 years. You can eat in the bar or dine in the stylish restaurant. Telephone: 01476 860035.

THE WALK

Buckminster has a tree-lined main street, and lies about ½ mile from the Lincolnshire border. Many of the properties in the village and local area are owned by the Buckminster Estates, who are linked with the Tollemache family who live in Buckminster Park, the former home of the Earl of Dysart. The village pub is situated in the High Street and is still called the Tollemache Arms. The church of St John the Baptist acts as a landmark, being visible for miles around, high on the Leicestershire Wolds.

From the church, descend to the left of the new residential building set to the right of the old manor house in **Buckminster**. You will be walking down part of the **Mowbray Way**. At the bottom of the hedged part of the footpath turn right over a stile and follow the waymarkers that lead you onto a footpath set to the left of the trees, initially part of **Parkside Wood**.

Walk to the left of the trees for the next mile. Pass by the entrance to the **Pony Camp** and continue along the clear footpath to the left of the trees, passing **Park Oaks** and **Bottom Plantation**. Eventually cross over a footbridge and bear left,

Along the way

Wild flowers add a splash of colour to the fields

then right, to continue along a clear farm track.

②

This track bends right and here you take the clear footpath that ascends a cultivated field up to a yellow marker post. Continue ahead up the wide clear track, going over the hill to arrive in the village of **Sproxton**.

The church in Sproxton stands to the north of the village and in the churchyard is said to be a 10th-century Saxon cross. From the end of the 19th century until the middle of the 20th century many local men were employed in ironstone mining at nearby Saltby Heath – a more profitable undertaking then than farming. St Bartholomew's parish church offers a peal of eight bells on Sundays.

 ③

Turn left and descend the lane into the village. At the road junction turn left and stroll down the pavement into the centre of the village. At the main road, turn left past the **Crown Inn** and up a lane called **The Nook**.

 ④

At its end turn left and then bear right into a mown area of land. At the end of the lawned area, go over the stile in the left-hand corner and ascend the bank up to the field hedge. Turn right and continue to the right of the hedge. Soon you will descend to a corner field stile. Cross over a footbridge before ascending the hill ahead. Follow the yellow-post route up to the lane.

 ⑤

Turn right and proceed along the lane passing the entrance to **Coston Lodge West**. At a bend turn left then keep ahead at a T-junction.

 ⑥

In about 300 yards, turn left onto a wide track across a cultivated field. Continue ahead, keeping to the left of the field hedge and walking a clear wide footpath. You pass the right-hand end of a small triangle of trees and will soon arrive on the road on the edge of **Buckminster** village.

 ⑦

Turn right and proceed up into the village, turning left along **Back Street** to arrive back outside the church parkland area.

PLACE OF INTEREST NEARBY

Naturescape Wild Flower Farm, north-west of Buckminster, at Coach Gap Lane, Langar, has 44 acres of wild flower fields to explore. The fields are alive with butterflies and bees. Free admission. Telephone: 01949 860592.

4 Old Dalby

The countryside around Old Dalby

The Walk 3 miles 🕐 2 hours
Map OS Explorer 246 Loughborough (GR 674236)

How to get there

Old Dalby is north-west of Melton and can be reached from either the A6006 or the A46 from Leicester. **Parking:** On Paradise Lane near the church.

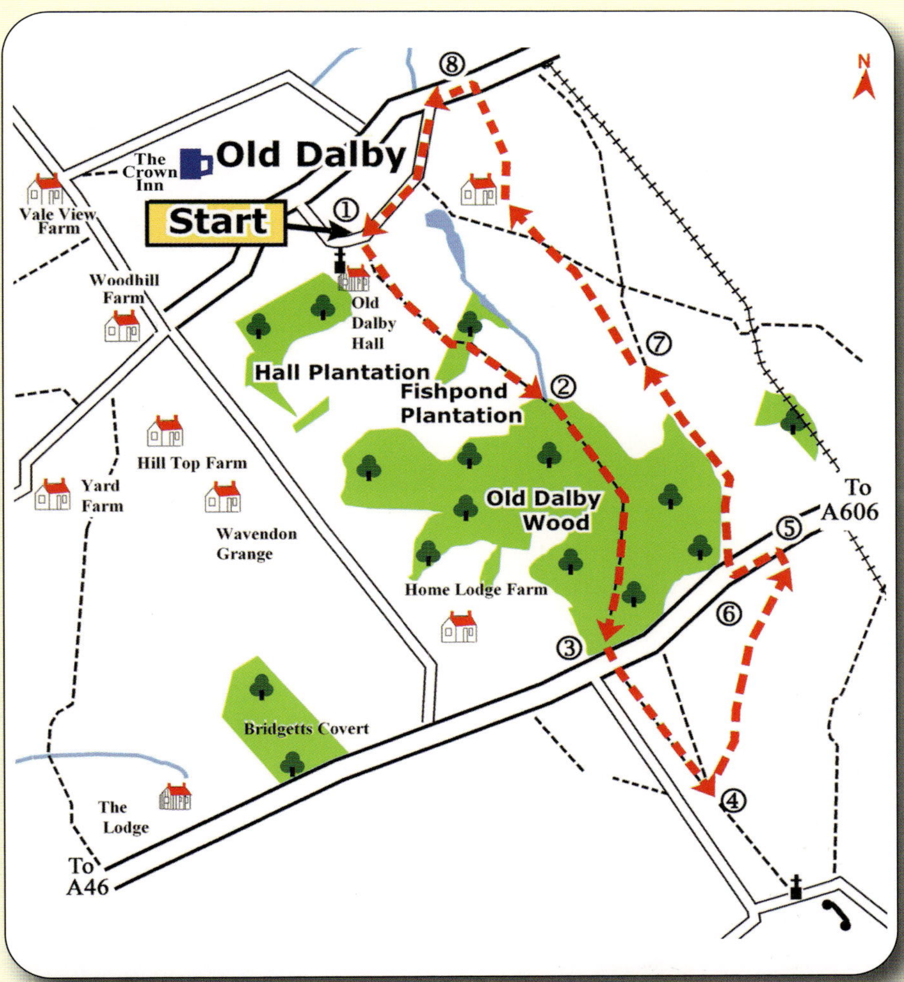

Introduction

Old Dalby is an historic village and the former control centre of British Rail's Research Division's railway test track between Melton Mowbray and Edwalton. This short, easy stroll takes you into the superb Old Dalby Wood, a fine bluebell wood in spring, when you should also see primroses and wood anemones. The route passes Old Dalby Hall and Fishpond Plantation, before looping back over this lovely area of countryside.

Refreshments

The 16th-century **Crown Inn** at Old Dalby is a real ale pub and offers a bar menu and evening meals served in the restaurant. Please note that the pub is closed all day Monday. Telephone: 01664 823134.

THE WALK

From the **church** in **Old Dalby**, descend **Paradise Lane** for a few yards, then turn right past the waymarked sign into a fishermen's car park. Continue through the small car parking area and go over the stile to proceed across pastureland towards **Fishpond Plantation** – you will see the fine building and the ha-ha at **Old Dalby Hall** to your right and will soon reach **Fishpond Plantation**. Enter the plantation via a stile, walk through and exit via a second stile. Now cross the next farm field to reach a hand gate that leads into **Old Dalby Wood**, which is a mass of bluebells in the spring.

Pass through the hand gate into the wood. Initially you will be

The church of St John the Baptist at Old Dalby

Old Dalby Hall seen at point 1 of the walk

walking on a public footpath and later join the forest track to continue. In about 100 yards look out for a public footpath going off to the right and continue up this. The footpath ascends and then levels off before rejoining the forest track as you near the end of the wood to reach a road.

 ③

At the wood end, cross the road and proceed over the stile opposite, walking the footpath that soon veers along by the left hedge. Presently you will see the yellow waymark post at the end of the pastureland and should aim for this. Go over the stile and turn left to go over a second stile.

 ④

Take the public footpath going to the left (north-east) along a clear footpath through the field. Go over the stile at its end and continue over the next field, aiming towards a further signed stile just outside a small electrical substation.

 ⑤

Go over the stile and turn left down a rather narrow fenced pathway to reach the road. Turn left and stroll along the road verge for about 100 yards.

 **6**

Cross over the road and proceed down the clear farm track that circles the edge of **Old Dalby Wood**, then arcs left to continue, with pleasing views ahead. In about 150 yards you will reach a track junction and here you take the left fork.

 **7**

Continue down this left track, descending generally towards a farm-type complex. The track takes you to the right of the buildings and eventually you will reach **Old Dalby Lane**.

 **8**

Turn left and proceed along the side of this approach lane to the village of **Old Dalby**. In about 100 yards turn left down **Paradise Lane** to arrive back at your car.

PLACE OF INTEREST NEARBY

Ragdale Hall Health Hydro and Thermal Spa in nearby Ragdale is just the place to pamper yourself. Telephone: 01664 434831.

5 Staunton Harold

Setting off

The Walk 6 miles 🕐 4 hours
Map OS Explorer 245 The National Forest (GR 378220)

How to get there

Staunton Harold is approximately 4 miles north of Ashby-de-la-Zouch near the border with Derbyshire. From the A42 between Nottingham and Ashby, turn west onto the B587. Staunton Harold is along a turning on the left. **Parking:** In the free car park at Staunton Harold.

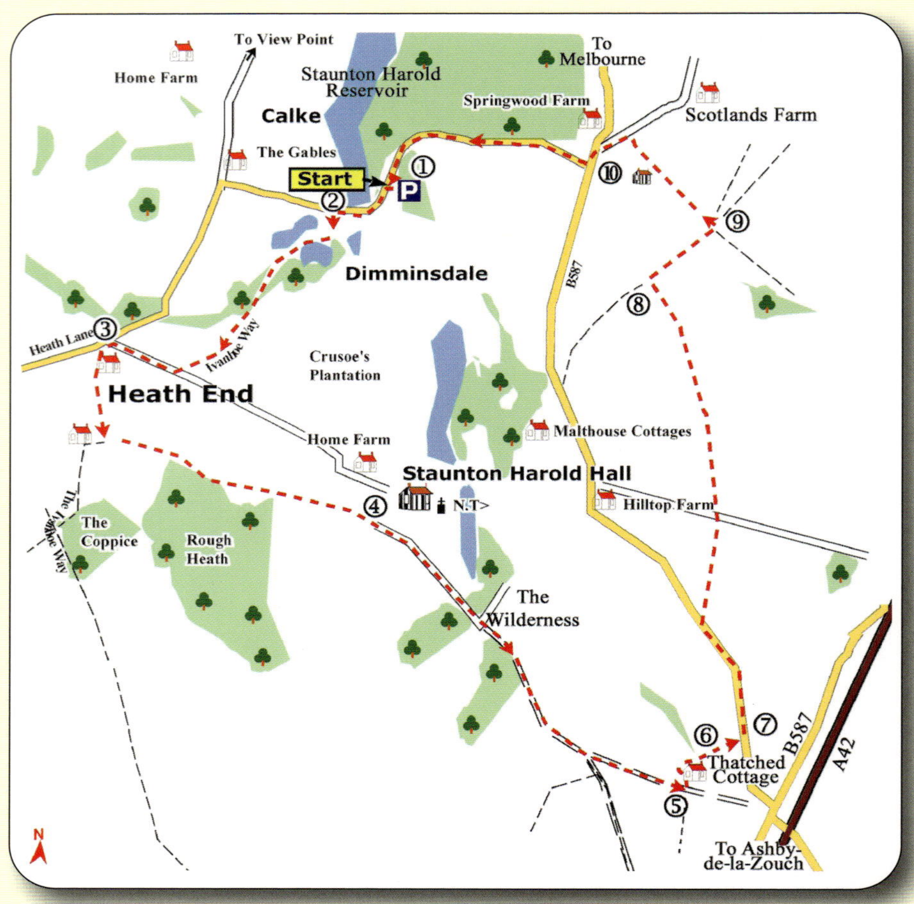

Introduction

This lovely walk takes you through beautiful wooded hills to visit the Staunton Harold Estate. From the tip of the Staunton Harold Reservoir you walk south on the Ivanhoe Way, and pass the private Staunton Harold Hall and its unique church before returning along lovely country paths.

Refreshments

Staunton Stables is a family-run tea room that serves delicious home-made food. Set in the Ferrers Centre for Arts and Crafts at Staunton Harold, this is a very pleasant place to stop and enjoy some refreshment. Telephone: 01332 864617.

THE WALK

Leave the car park and turn left to stroll down the road and cross over the water of the **Staunton Harold reservoir**.

In about 50 yards turn left (you will be in Derbyshire initially) and stroll down the footpath of the **Ivanhoe Way**. You pass a couple of notice-boards and continue along the **Way**, passing two reservoirs. The route takes you up some steps and then turns right over a stile to continue along the **Ivanhoe Way**. Leave the woodland via a further stile to arrive at a lane in **Heath End**. Exit right onto the road and turn left when you reach a T-junction.

The Ivanhoe Way is a 35-mile long-distance path that starts and ends at Shackerstone, and can take you around the north-western area of the Leicestershire countryside, including Charnwood Forest. The route links with the Leicestershire Round.

In about 20 yards, turn left again and enter the garden of a large house, keeping to the grass verge by the side of the house drive. Exit at the rear of the house onto a lane. Here, turn left and stroll up the lane past some attractive houses. In about 150 yards, you leave the **Ivanhoe Way** turning left over a stile along a public footpath and stroll across farm fields, passing through a kissing gate and a couple of metal kissing gates, as you walk past the woodland of **Rough Heath**. If you keep to the waymarked footpath, you will soon arrive near to the buildings of **Staunton Harold Hall** and **church**.

Staunton was mentioned in the Domesday Book as being held by Henry de Ferrers, and remained in the Ferrers family until it was sold in 1954. The house was largely rebuilt by Sir Robert Shirley, the 1st Earl of Ferrers, in 1653. He also built the adjoining church (now managed by the National Trust) in 1653. Over the door can be read: 'In the year 1653 when all things sacred were throughout the nation either demolished or profaned, Sir Robert Shirley, Baronet founded this church; whose singular praise it is to have done the best things in the worst times and hoped them in the most calamitous. The righteous shall be had in everlasting remembrance.'

Washington Shirley, who became the 5th Earl Ferrers, rebuilt the hall in the present Palladian style to

An attractive thatched cottage passed on the route

which was added later the Georgian front. Staunton House was saved from demolition by Group Captain Lord Cheshire, VC, to become one of his homes for the incurably sick, then, later, it became a Sue Ryder home. Now the house is the private residence of the Blunt family. It houses frequent exhibitions by local artists, a café and a shop. Behind the house is the Ferrers Craft Centre, which evolved from a pottery established here in 1974. There are also nurseries and a large garden centre stocking the usual garden sundries, as well as some unusual trees and shrubs and an aquatic section.

 ④

Turn right and continue down the road past the Hall. Continue along this good road for about 150 yards then, where the road bends left, continue ahead through a brown-painted hand gate by a yellow waymark stake onto a clear wide track. Proceed along this track for about 250 yards, bearing left at the junction of paths.

 ⑤

In a further 200 yards turn left over a stile and pass to the left of a very attractive thatched cottage. Exit onto the road by the cottage and head right for about 20 yards.

Turn left and cross farm fields to reach a lane.

Turn left along the lane and stroll along its grass verge for about 250 yards. When you have reached the end of **Lawn Plantation**, cross the road and enter the footpath opposite, following the direction of the waymarker. This will lead you along the left of the field hedge over several fields and stiles as you cross a wide track, going in a northerly direction.

At the end of the third large field look for and go right over the stile in its far corner. This will take you along the left edge of a large field. Go over the stile in the corner end, then turn left over another stile in the hedge.

Cross the large farm field, turning left, and aiming for another stile situated by a yellow marker post. Now ascend to the right of a thatched cottage and exit onto the road opposite **Springwood Farm**.

Turn left, cross the B587 road and then turn right along the road to **Calke**. Proceed along this road for about 450 yards and you will arrive back at the **Staunton Harold car park**.

PLACE OF INTEREST NEARBY

Two miles to the north-west is **Calke Abbey**, a baroque mansion set in a stunning landscaped park. The house contains the spectacular natural history collection of the Harpur Crewe family. It is owned by the National Trust. Telephone 01332 863822 or log on to www.nationaltrust.org.uk for opening times and admission prices.

6 Walton on the Wolds and Prestwold Hall

The clear path through the trees

The Walk 4 miles ⏱ 3 hours
Map OS Explorer 246 Loughborough (GR 593198)

How to get there

Walton on the Wolds is just 3 miles east of Loughborough. From Loughborough, take the A60 and follow the B676 and then the B675 to Walton. **Parking:** By the green in the village, near to the Anchor Inn.

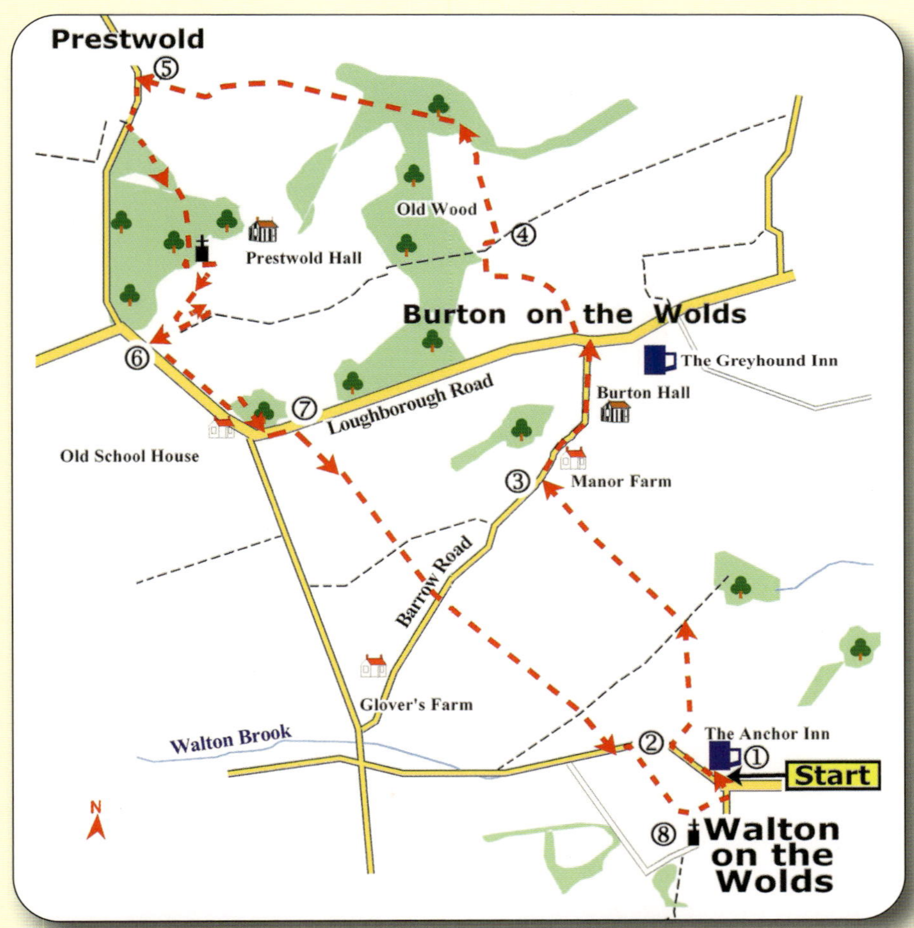

Introduction

This is a pleasing stroll around Walton on the Wolds, passing through Burton on the Wolds and the delightful Prestwold Hall Park, with good views of the Hall.

Refreshments

The **Anchor Inn** in Walton on the Wolds is a freehouse that offers bar food, as well as a full menu. Please note that the pub is closed on Monday lunchtime. Telephone: 01509 880018.

THE WALK

Walton on the Wolds is a tiny village with a population of around 250 persons. In the 19th century it was the home of Augustus Hobart-Hampden, better known as Hobart Pasha, who had an adventurous naval career. After service in the Crimea, he became a blockade-runner in the American Civil War (using the alias of Captain Roberts). In more recent times the village has been used as a location for the TV series, Boon, starring Neil Morrissey, with the Tudor house, Kings Cote, doubling as Boon's house.

From the parking area near the green, descend the **Main Street**, passing the **Anchor Inn** and the **Old Manor House**.

In about 100 yards, turn sharp right to go over a stile (just before reaching **May Cottage**) and walk a hedged footpath to reach open land. Go over the stile and footbridge to continue up towards **Manor Farm** – you will pass by a sewage works (over the hedge) to walk along a tarmac driveway to the sewage works. **Burton Hall** can be seen to the right.

Turn right along **Barrow Road** and stroll past the entrance to **Manor Farm** as you descend into the village of **Burton on the Wolds**.

Burton on the Wolds is a small village with a population of around 800. It has its own primary school, pub (the Greyhound) and shop (located in the garage). The village is famous for its Lion's Head fountain.

When you reach the road island in the middle of the village, cross the road and proceed down a signed and hedged footpath to reach **Seymour Road**.

Turn left and stroll along towards the end of **Seymour Road**. Now continue along the clear waymarked footpath set to the left of a field hedge – it appears to go towards **Old Wood** but just before reaching it turn right and proceed through a farm gate.

The footpath will take you along the side of the wood. Turn right at the field corner before going left to cross a footbridge. Now ascend and cross a cultivated field, aiming for the yellow waymarked footpath by the trees. Proceed along the footpath that soon follows the fence line. Eventually you will emerge in **Prestwold Park** and should continue along the clear footpath set to the right edge of the park until you reach an entrance gate.

The impressive Prestwold Hall

 ⑤

Turn right over the cattle grid to exit the park, then turn left and walk along the grass verge of the **Nottingham road**. In about 100 yards, when opposite to an old 1834 building, cross the road and enter the park on a waymarked footpath. The clear footpath will take you around the left-hand edge of trees and then the footpath veers to the right of the church which belongs to the estate. The footpath continues at the back of the church and bears left, then goes right towards an entrance gate. After zig-zagging, the path reaches the **Nottingham road** once again via an entrance gate.

⑥

Turn left and walk the clear footpath set inside the trees. This will eventually bend left for you to enjoy a rather special view of **Prestwold Hall**.

Prestwold Hall is a magnificent private house, largely remodelled in 1843 by William Burn. It contains fine Italian plasterwork, and 18th-century English and European furniture. For the past 350 years it has been the home of the Packe family. Although not open to the general public the Hall has become a popular conference and corporate entertainment venue. Some 20 acres of gardens provide a perfect setting and marquees are often used for larger meetings. Activity days are available for clay pigeon shooting, motor sports and archery.

The footpath then bends right back into the trees and will eventually emerge on **Loughborough Road**. Go left along the road for about 50 yards.

 (7)

Now cross the road and proceed over the stile by another yellow-painted post. Cross the cultivated field to a further yellow post and go left and then right to continue along the very clear footpath. You will be walking in a generally south-easterly direction over the fields towards the village of **Walton on the Wolds**. After walking over several fields the path turns right and you will emerge in the village on **Walton Lane**. Turn left and cross the lane to go right over a stile and ascend through the trees with new houses to your left and fields to the right.

 (8)

At the top of the footpath the route bends left past houses to arrive near to the church in **Walton on the Wolds**. Eventually you will reach the **Loughborough Road**. Turn left and you will soon find refreshments and your car near to the **Anchor Inn** in **Walton on the Wolds**.

The church at point 5 of the walk

PLACE OF INTEREST NEARBY

Belvoir Castle, 6½ miles north, is a magnificent building and well worth a visit. Telephone: 01476 871004; www.belvoircastle.com (see Walk 1)

7 Cossington, the River Soar and the Grand Union Canal

The Grand Union Canal

The Walk 4¼ miles 🕐 Allow 2 to 3 hours
Map OS Explorer 246 Loughborough (GR 604133)

How to get there

Cossington can be reached from the A6 north of Leicester. Turn east off the A6 onto the B5328 at Rothley. **Parking:** In the free car park at the recreation ground near Cossington sports field.

Introduction

Enjoy an easy stroll around attractive Cossington village and meander along the towpath of the Grand Union Canal to experience the history of the canal system. The walk continues along the banks of the River Soar to the mill at Sileby before returning on part of the Leicestershire Round walking route.

Refreshments

The **Royal Oak** in Cossington offers an interesting international cuisine. Telephone: 01509 813937.

THE WALK

From the car park, proceed through the kissing gate onto the sports field. Cross this aiming for a yellow waymarker post opposite – take care not to damage the pitches or the cricket square. Walk the clear path which soon emerges onto a road almost opposite **Cossington Grange**. Head right along the road for about 125 yards.

Turn left opposite to a lane junction and walk a clear path going generally south, passing by two very attractive lakes. In about 440 yards you will arrive on the towpath of the **Grand Union Canal** near to **Junction Lock**.

The Grand Union Canal is part of the British canal system connecting London and Birmingham and stretches for 137 miles. It has 166 locks. It was also the original name for part of what is now known as the Leicester Line of the modern Grand Union.

Turn right and walk the lovely towpath, passing by **Cossington Lock** (where the **River Soar** joins the canal) before ascending a bridge to arrive on a road near to **Cossington Old Mill**.

Cross over the road, bearing left then right, descending to the towpath to continue on the opposite bank of the canal. Stroll along the towpath that initially draws near to the noisy A6 road but then pulls away. The canal is like a wide river and you are likely to see a number of colourful narrowboats and fishermen trying to catch their supper. The attractive towpath walk draws to an end shortly after you pass by a pipe bridge, when you reach and cross over a series of canal bridges at **Sileby Mill**.

The old mill at Sileby was built in 1608 but has now been restored as a private residence. Sileby was a thriving community based around the hosiery-manufacturing trade before becoming swollen with dormitory housing for Leicester and Loughborough.

Just after crossing over the second of the canal footbridges, bear right to join the **Leicestershire Round** walking path. Stroll down the 'Round' route back towards the village of **Cossington**. The path veers south initially along the other bank of the canal, passing a row of fishermen's numbered positions.

At the end of the third large field, turn left, walking to the right of the hedge with gravel works to your

Cossington Old Mill

right. After walking the path over two fields and stiles, bear right (south-east) and the village of **Cossington** becomes visible. Go over a stile to the left of a large farm gate and stroll along the wide track towards the village – a pair of metal kissing gates lead you to the main street and you pass through the edge of the churchyard. Spare time to walk around this pretty village with wide, well-kept grass verges and an abundance of trees.

 (7)

When you have had your fill of Cossington, return to the track and the large farm gate. Now leave the **Leicestershire Round** by turning left through a kissing gate and stroll along the edge of a very attractive old moat where yellow irises and water lilies produce a scene of beauty in spring. At the end of the moat area, head south over a stile into trees and you will soon arrive back on the road near to the car park.

PLACE OF INTEREST NEARBY

The **National Space Centre** at Leicester (5 miles south of Cossington) is the UK's largest attraction dedicated to space science. Here you will be treated to hours of breathtaking discovery and interactive fun. Telephone: 01162 610261; www.spacecentre.co.uk

8 Exton and Exton Park

Exton church

The Walk 4½ miles ⏱ 3 hours
Map OS Explorer 234 Rutland Water (GR 925113)

How to get there

Exton is 2 miles north of Rutland Water and can be reached via the A606 Oakham-Stamford road. **Parking:** Around the green in Exton.

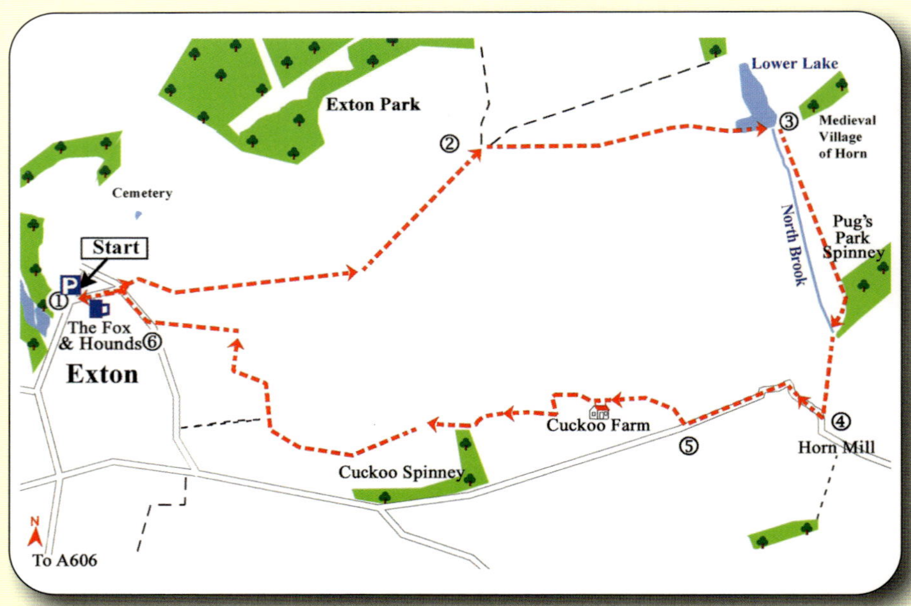

Introduction

Exton is a beautiful village with a tree-planted green overlooked by the Fox & Hounds pub, and this lovely stroll takes you around the village and into the surrounding countryside, past a lake, to see the attractive trout hatchery at Horn Mill. Wild flowers are abundant along the way, especially on the return route through a gentle valley.

Refreshments

The **Fox & Hounds** in Exton is a lovely former coaching inn with a splendid walled garden. Telephone: 01572 812403.

THE WALK

Cross over and leave **the green** to walk Exton's handsome **High Street**, going right – north-east. The High Street is lined with a long row of terraced thatched cottages and you pass the church on your left. Bear right at the end of the street into **Top Street** and then **Stamford Road/Empingham Road**, and then go left up **Newfield Road** where you will pass a number of attractive modern houses as you leave the village. Continue over the cattle grid on the tarmac track and descend through an attractive landscape that is the result of disused mine workings – to your left you will see tarmac tracks.

 ②

Turn right and carry on along the track, which becomes a soil/stone track as it continues to gently descend to go over a stile/gate by **Lower Lake**. As you cross the dam end of this beautiful lake you will, in season, pass yellow irises planted at the water's edge. On the lake, you are likely to see swans, Canada geese, coots and moorhens, and probably fishermen on the banks.

 ③

At the dam end turn right onto a waymarked path going generally south/south-east. After going over a further stile, you will see **Horn House** on the hill to your left and below it you can look out for the remains of the medieval village of **Horn**. Continue to the left of the hedge/fence with **North Brook** to your right until you reach **Pug's Park Spinney**. When you reach a sign into the woods stating 'Private (Exton Estates)', bear right to go over a concrete farm bridge across the brook and climb to a stile. Go over the stile and walk the clear stone track by the field edge which leads you past the trout hatchery to a stile onto a quiet lane.

The town pump in Exton

 ④

Turn right and stroll along the lane for about ¾ mile. In spring you will enjoy seeing wild flowers along the roadside verge.

⑤

At the waymark post, turn right over a stile and proceed north/north-west on a fairly steep, short descent to go over a second stile and a footbridge across a brook from **Hawkswell Spring**. Walk the pleasant clear path to the right of the brook, passing by **Cuckoo Farm**, and then go over a further stile and footbridge to the other side of the brook. You will walk a gentle valley with wild flowers covering the banks, eventually going over a stile into the bottom end of **Cuckoo Spinney**. Leave the spinney via another stile and proceed over a footbridge to now walk the north side of the brook on the wild flower valley walk. Continue for approximately a further 500 yards. At the end of the spinney go over a couple of stiles then bear right (north) up a hedged/fenced wide path that zigzags past school playing fields to emerge by trees. Here, turn left and stroll past the school buildings to reach a road.

The delightful village pub in Exton

 **6**

Proceed along the road until you arrive back in **Empingham Road** in Exton. Turn right and as the road bends left, go left past some very beautiful thatched cottages to reach the green opposite the **Fox & Hounds Inn** in the centre of the village.

PLACES OF INTEREST NEARBY

Exton is such a beautiful village that you should take to time to explore it closely. Exton Park is a large country estate which has been home to the Noel family (Earls of Gainsborough) for over four centuries. The present **Exton Hall** was built in the 19th century close to the ruins of the original Tudor mansion which had burnt down in 1810 and contains a Roman Catholic chapel. The grand **parish church of St Peter and St Paul** lies on the edge of the park and contains an impressive collection of monuments. The romantic **Fort Henry** is a pleasure house built in the late 18th-century Gothic style and is situated overlooking the lakes formed by the North Brook. Information is available from www.rutnet.co.uk/exton

9 A Measham Meander

The lake in Willesley Wood

The Walk 4½ miles 🕐 3 hours
Map OS Explorer 245 The National Forest (GR 324134)

How to get there

The walk starts at the National Forest car park outside Oakthorpe, on the B586 south-west of Ashby-de-la-Zouch. **Parking:** In the free National Forest car park.

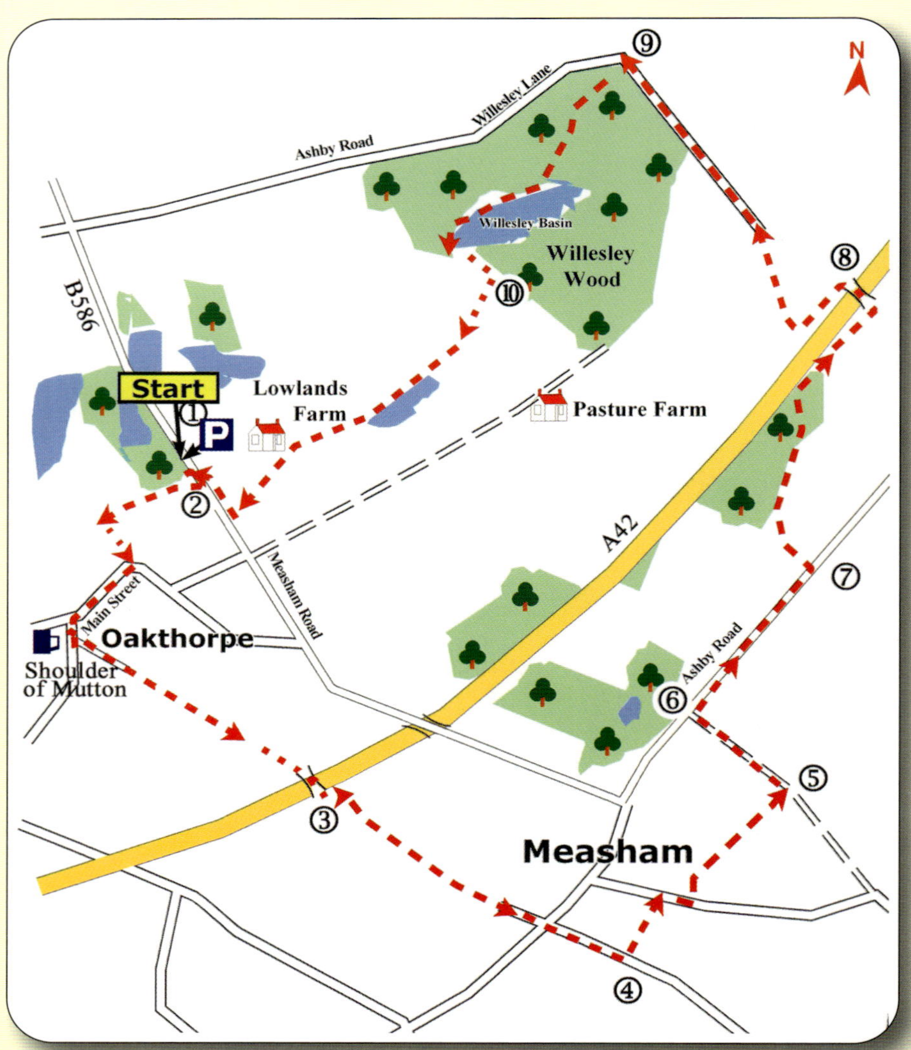

Introduction

This lovely walk is through beautiful wooded countryside to Measham, returning through Willesley Wood with its picturesque lake. The village of Measham lies near the heart of the National Forest, situated close to the Staffordshire and Derbyshire borders. It was originally a small market town, although it was dismissed by William Wyrley in 1596 as 'a village belonging to Lord Shefield, in which are many coal mines, [but] little else worthy of remembrance'.

Refreshments

The **Shoulder of Mutton** in Oakthorpe is a popular local, serving good food in pleasant surroundings. Telephone: 01530 270436.

THE WALK

Leave the **National Forest car park** and proceed onto the main road, heading right, up the side of the busy B586 road.

In about 50 yards turn right again. Go over the stile and proceed along the pleasant hedged footpath. After going over a second stile you will soon reach a farm gate. Go over the stile to its right and stroll up to the road. Turn left and ascend **Canal Road** to reach **Main Street**, in **Oakthorpe**. Turn right and descend the road, turning left up a dead-end road called **Silver Street** – you will see the **Shoulder of Mutton** public house ahead to the right of the street. At its end continue ahead and proceed into open countryside on a footpath set to the left of the field hedge. Continue ahead through the hedge gap and stroll to the end of the next field. Now bear right to proceed around the edge of the field and descend right down towards a footbridge over the A42.

Once over the footbridge, turn sharp left and then go right down a clear footpath set to the right of a field hedge. At the bottom of this footpath bear left and follow the waymark direction along a quiet road. Soon you will reach the **High Street** in **Measham**.

St Laurence parish church is situated off the Main Street and it has a West tower from the 1730s and 14th-century windows.

Some 1¼ miles east is the mid-Georgian seven-bay house called Measham Hall. Joseph Wilkes was a prominent figure in the history of Measham. He was an entrepreneur during the early part of the Industrial Revolution and bought Measham manor from William Wollaston in 1777. He undertook extensive industrial and agricultural development of the village. He used larger bricks (enlarged to twice the standard size) in much of his architecture in order to reduce the tax on the manufacture of such bricks (tax was proportional to the number of bricks used in building).

The footbridge that leads you back to Measham

A type of pottery known as Meashamware is named after the village, although it was actually produced in Derbyshire at Church Gresley. Until about 1897 Measham was, in fact, merely an enclave of Derbyshire.

 ④

Turn left and then go right up **Leicester Road** for about 300 yards. When opposite the school buildings, cross the road and ascend the clear signed footpath that will lead you into open countryside. Diagonally cross the farm field and then proceed up the next field until you arrive at a grassy lane (path).

 ⑤

Turn left, then stroll up this green lane and soon you will arrive at the B5006 Ashby road.

 ⑥

Turn right and proceed up the pavement for about 500 yards.

 ⑦

Turn left up a clear hedged track. Just before the track enters woodland turn right up a signed footpath and continue up this until you arrive at the bridge crossing over the busy A42 road once again.

 ⑧

Turn left along the clear wide

footpath that runs parallel with the A42 for about 200 yards. The path then bends right and soon you will be walking along a tarmac road. This descends and then gently ascends until you reach a junction of roads.

 **⑨**

Turn left through a gateway gap and descend the delightful path into **Willesley Wood**. In about ½ mile you will be walking near to **Willesley Basin**. The path continues beyond the Basin as you circle left along a good stone footpath. The path bends left and then right and you will exit the woodland via a stile.

Willesley Wood is a beautiful 140-acre Woodland Trust site. In the middle of the wood is Willesley Basin, dug out about 200 years ago as a boating lake for the Hastings family who owned nearby Willesley Hall. Today it is a private fishing lake stocked with carp, pike and tench. The surrounding wetland fringes are important to amphibians and water fowl.

 **⑩**

Continue ahead (left) along the clear wide footpath. The path reaches a junction of paths but you go ahead over a stile and continue along a good footpath passing through woodland and soon you will see a lake through the trees to your left. As you continue you pass near to **Lowlands Farm** (on the right). The footpath takes you to the left of a cottage and over a stile and onto the road once again. Turn right and stroll down the side of the road, which you cross over to get back to the **National Forest car park**.

PLACE OF INTEREST NEARBY

Conkers, 4 miles north of Measham, offers a unique mix of indoor and outdoor experiences for the whole family. There is woodland to explore, as well as lakes and gardens, plus interactive displays in the Discovery and Waterside Centres. Telephone: 01283 216633. Website: www.visitconkers.com.

10 Bradgate Park and Old John

The deer park

The Walk 3¾ miles ⏱ 3 hours
Map OS Explorer 246 Loughborough (GR 522117)

How to get there

Bradgate Park is approximately 7 miles north-west of Leicester and can be accessed from the B5327 at Newtown Linford. **Parking:** In the park and ride car park at Hunters End.

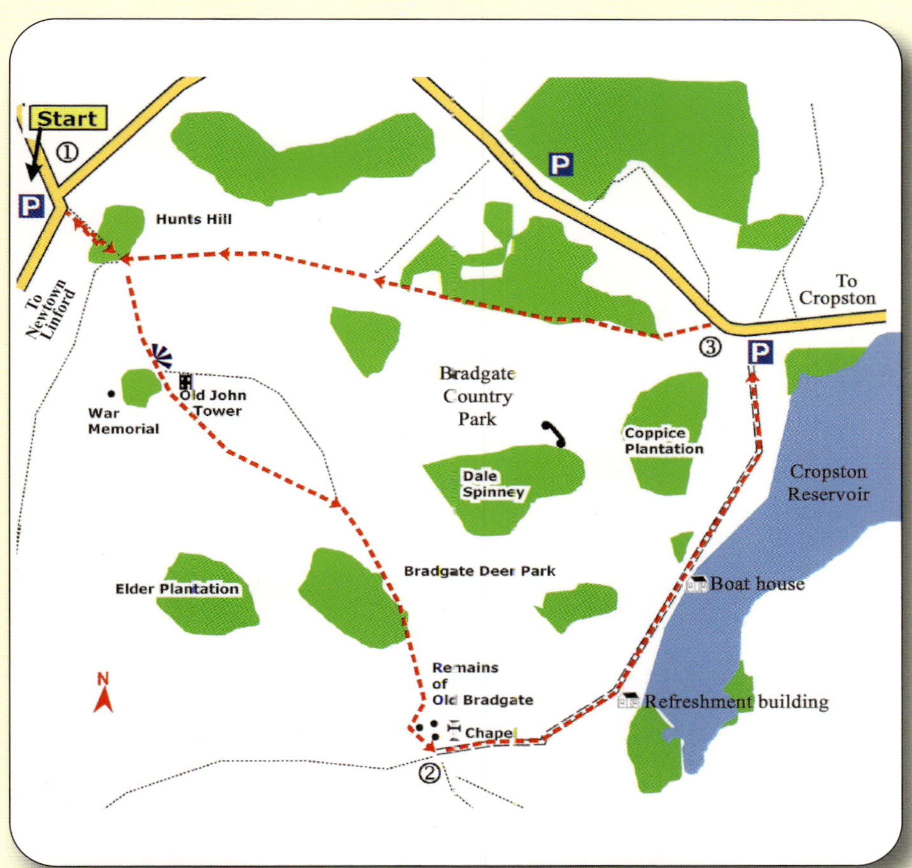

Introduction

This superb walk in Bradgate Park, where you are likely to see deer at play, takes you past the Old John folly, the war memorial and along the side of a beautiful reservoir.

The Greys of Groby owned Bradgate until 1926 when Charles Bennion (a director of British United Shoe Company) bought and presented it to the people of Leicestershire, a 1,000-acre time capsule of landscape preserved in a remarkable wild state. It is an historic medieval deer park in the heart of the ancient Charnwood Forest. It retains much of its original landscape with small woods, grassy slopes and rocky outcrops. Red and fallow deer can still be seen feeding amidst the bracken.

Refreshments

These are available at the **Bradgate Park Deer Barn Tea Room** on the edge of Cropston reservoir in the park itself. Telephone: 01162 362713.

THE WALK

From the car park, enter **Bradgate Country Park** and ascend the hill towards Old John, pausing to take in the scene.

Old John is a folly sited at the top of the highest hill in Bradgate Park. It was built in 1784 by the Grey family, and was originally an observation tower to give the ladies a view of a racecourse which circled the top of the hill. It is well known for its 'mug-shape', the 'handle' of which was added later, apparently in memory of a beer-loving family retainer. In the past, Old John was also used as a meeting place for hunters with their foxhounds, and a luncheon house for shooting parties in the park. Prince Albert's Own Leicestershire Yeomanry Regimental War Memorial is sited on the same mound as Old John, overlooking Leicester and the Soar valley.

Descend the footpath on the other side of the hill, passing to the left of woodland and through **Bradgate deer park**, and emerging to the right of the remains of **Old Bradgate**.

Bradgate Park was cleared by the

Greys of Groby in the 15th century and the construction of Bradgate House was begun in 1490 by Sir John Grey, 7th Baron Ferrers of Groby, the husband of Elizabeth Woodville. Old Bradgate was the birthplace of Lady Jane Grey, later Queen, ruling for a mere nine days before being overthrown by Mary I.

Bear left and pass by the old chapel pausing to see the deer. As you progress along the metalled track you will pass by the **Deer Barn Tea**

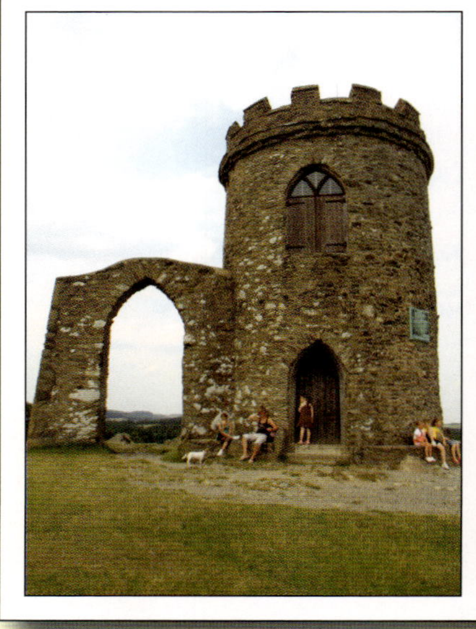

The Old John folly – a good place to rest and admire the view

On the way to Old Bradgate

Room and then the old **Boat House** by the edge of **Cropston Reservoir** and all too soon will arrive at a car parking area.

Cropston reservoir contains 500,000,000 gallons of water which is pumped into service reservoirs, and from these Leicester and the surrounding area is supplied by gravitation. The daily consumption is about 3,000,000 gallons, of which half comes from Cropston.

 ③

Pass through the car park and proceed onto the road. Turn left and walk up the side of the road for about 100 yards, then turn left at a waymarked footpath. This will lead you past a residential property. Bear right to enter the woodland of **Hallgate Hill Spinney**. Proceed up the clear footpath (watch out because horses are allowed up here) set along the left-hand edge of the spinney. This is a steady ascent but soon you will be leaving the trees and descending a hedged footpath with pleasing views to either side. As you approach the woodland on **Hunts Hill** you will get a good view of the **Old John**. Turn right and go over the hill before descending back to the car park.

11 Hungarton

The superb Quenby Hall

How to get there

Hungarton can be found off the A47, west of Leicester and north of Houghton on the Hill. **Parking:** In Church Lane, opposite the church in Hungarton.

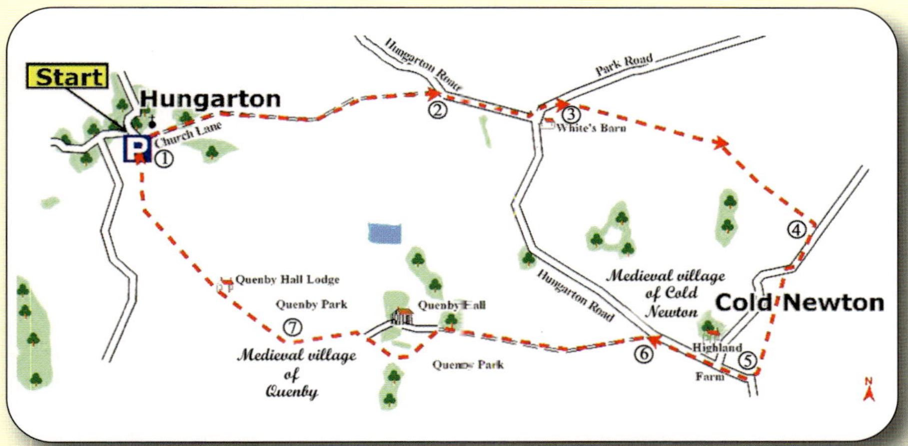

Introduction

A lovely stroll from an 18th-century model village, along peaceful country paths, to see two deserted medieval sites and pass Quenby Hall, an unspoiled jewel of a High Jacobean country house – the finest in Leicestershire and one of only a handful of such houses remaining in the UK.

Hungarton itself is a small village located approximately 10 miles from Leicester, with a church, a village hall, a small stream and a millennium green. The name is believed to have come from the Old English meaning 'hungry town'; it was called this because the quality of the soil in the area was so poor. The layout today follows that of the model village built between 1764 and 1776 by Shuckburgh Ashby, of the Ashby family of Quenby Hall.

Refreshments

The **Black Boy pub** in Hungarton has a reputation for good food. Telephone: 01162 595410.

THE WALK

From where you park your car, continue down **Church Lane**, bearing left. You will pass to the

right of farm buildings and then proceed through a bridlegate into woodland. A dirt track leads through the trees and you will emerge into farm grassland. Initially you bear left and then walk to the right of the farm hedge to continue along the bridlepath. This leads into a field and you should easily be able to follow the clear footpath as it continues over a large field. Continue on this footpath until you reach a hand gate onto the road.

 ②

Turn right and stroll along the road for about 200 yards when you will reach a junction of roads with **White's Barn** opposite. Turn left and then in about 100 yards you arrive at a point where the **Midshires Way** crosses the road.

 ③

Turn right and join the **Way**, going generally west. You will cross a farm field and descend to a stile by a farm gate. Go over this and continue up the left side of the next hedge. At the field end you arrive by a farm gate. Bear right through this, then go left through a new metal gate into more farmland. Aim for the metal gateway in the bottom of the field and from here the Way will take you up to a road on the outskirts of the village of **Cold Newton**.

 ④

Turn right up the road and stroll along this towards the village. At the sharp right bend, prior to reaching the village, bear left up a bridlepath to a gateway. Go through this and walk to the left of field hedges with the village off to your right. You will see a large house to your left and then pass an old moat area on the

other side of the hedge. Soon you descend to reach a bridlegate by a farm gate. Go through this rather awkward gate onto the roadway and turn right.

 ⑤

The road leads you past a right turn up into the village and as you ascend the next hill you will see an entrance gateway on your left.

 ⑥

Turn left and proceed up this good bridlepath that leads towards **Quenby Hall**. After passing through another bridlegate you will approach the buildings and get diverted around to the left of the Hall's wall. Rejoin the lane to the Hall at the other side of the building and continue along this to a lodge gate.

Quenby Hall was built in 1627 and many of the rooms are the same as they were when the architect conceived them, with beautiful proportions, intricate plaster ceilings, finely worked panelling and fireplaces. It has the advantage of presenting a spectacular face to the world whilst being of a manageable size. Quenby's great claim to international fame is that Stilton cheese was first made there, by the housekeeper. Her daughter lived at the staging inn at Stilton, and sold her mother's cheeses. The Hall is now the home of the de Lisle family whose ancestry in England dates back to the Norman conquest of

1066 – they have lived in Leicestershire for over 300 years. The superb building was built by George Ashby, passing out of the Ashby family's hands at the turn of the 20th century. It was bought in 1904 and restored by Lady Henry Grosvenor, who made many Edwardian improvements and restored much of the Jacobean interior after it had been 'georgianised' by Shuckburgh Ashby in the mid-18th century.

In 1922 it was bought by Sir Harold Nutting, who lived and hunted happily there for 50 years until his death in 1972: the Queen of Denmark, Princess Alice, Duchess of Gloucester and David Niven were among those who stayed here during this era. The Squire de Lisle then bought Quenby, to replace the family seat at Garendon Hall, which was demolished in 1964. Quenby has been extensively restored but remains faithful to its Jacobean heritage.

 ⑦

Here go through the entrance gateway and head sharp right over a stile to walk a clear footpath towards the village of **Hungarton** set on the hill opposite. When you reach the path junction, turn right and cross over a stream via a bridge, then head over the pastureland descending towards another stream bridge to reach a hand gate that will lead you back up into the village. You will return to **Church Lane** via a narrow tarmac footpath.

12 Bosworth Battlefield Walk

Enjoying a cruise on the Ashby Canal

The Walk 1¾ miles Allow 2 to 3 hours
Map OS Explorer 232 Nuneaton & Tamworth (GR 397004)

How to get there

The walk starts at Shenton railway station close to the Battlefield Heritage Centre, west of the A447 to the north of Hinckley. **Parking:** In the fee-paying car park at the station.

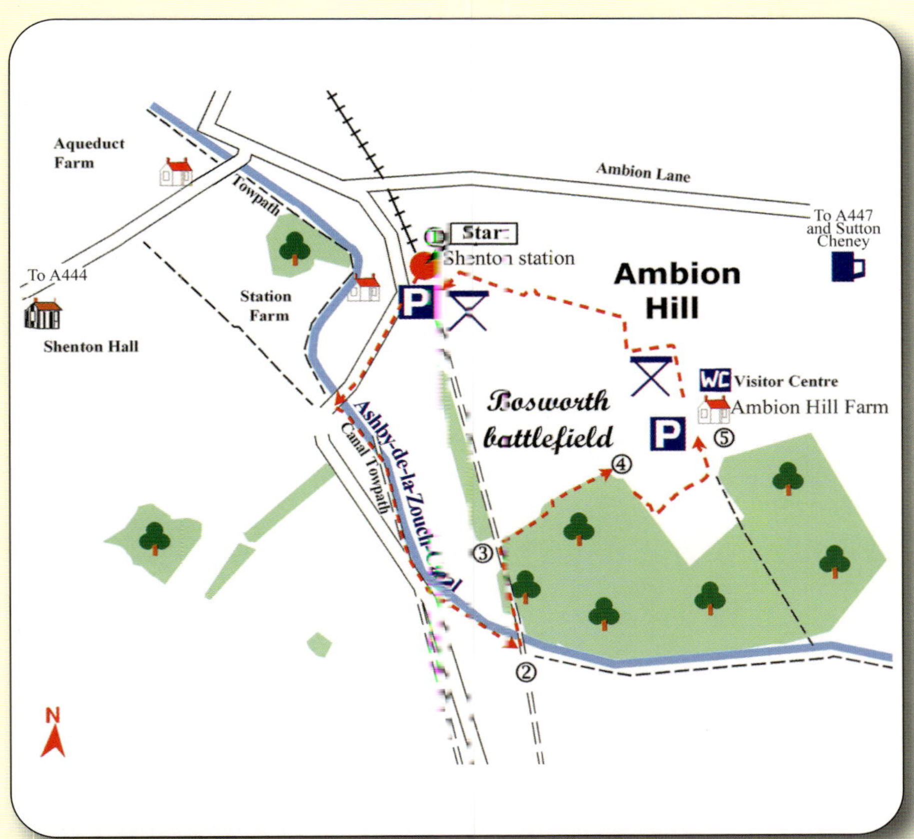

Introduction

This is a short, easy walk around the famous Bosworth battlefield. From Shenton railway station, preserved as part of the Battlefield Line, the route follows the towpath of the colourful Ashby-de-la-Zouch Canal before turning onto the battlefield site.

The Battle of Bosworth was one of the most influential in England's history. On 22nd August 1485 a rebel force defeated a royal army more than twice its size, leaving Richard III, the last Plantagenet king, dead on the field and placing Henry VII on the throne as the first of a new Tudor dynasty. This was the very last great medieval battle and the final battle of the Wars of the Roses – everyone remembers Shakespeare's poetic line for King Richard: 'A horse! A horse! My kingdom for a horse!'

Refreshments

The **Hercules Inn** in Sutton Cheney is a delightful 400-year-old coaching inn only 2 miles from the battlefield. Telephone: 01455 292591.

Refreshments are also available at the **Battlefield Heritage Centre**. Telephone: 01455 290429.

THE WALK

①

Leave **Shenton station** and stroll down the very quiet lane going south-west. In about 400 yards, cross **Bridge No 35** over the **Ashby Canal**.

②

Go immediately left through a hand gate to join the canal towpath. As you walk along the towpath, yellow iris plants are a treat in spring and colourful narrow-boats contribute to an idyllic scene.

③

In about 750 yards you leave the towpath through a wooden hand gate by an old metal-sided railway bridge and turn left, crossing over the wooden planked bridge to a gravel footpath just inside **Ambion Woods** – a pleasant tree-lined path. In about 500 yards, bear right and ascend away from the main footpath that bends to reach a hand gate near a sign: '**Ambion Wood**'. Proceed north-east inside the wood edge. You will pass signs – 'The Marsh' and 'Richard's Left Flank' – which reveal the layout of the Bosworth battlefield.

④

At the wood end you will reach **Richard's Well**, which displays a Latin inscription that translates thus:

Richard III, King of England slaked his thirst with water drawn from this well, when engaged in most bitter and furious battle with Henry, Earl of Richmond and before being deprived of both his life and his sceptre on the morning of 22 August AD 1485.

⑤

Proceed through the metal hand gate at the back of the well and stroll up to the **Battlefield Heritage Centre**, where you can find out more about the events of that day.

Richard's Well

One of the old railway buildings at Shenton station

It is well worth taking time to visit the Heritage Centre. For opening times and admission prices, telephone 01455 290429; www.bosworthbattlefield.com The Battlefield Line which runs from Shenton Station to Shackerstone is the last remaining part of the former Ashby & Nuneaton Joint Railway which was opened in 1873. It is operated by the Shackerstone Railway Society.

⑤

Leave the centre and follow the sign to **Shenton station** by aiming for the top right-hand corner at the end of the parking area. Walk along the good path that meanders down the slope to reach the station. You will pass by a series of battlefield signs which well illustrate the extent of the battleground in 1485: 'King Richard's Vanguard', 'Richard's Command Position', 'Northumberland's Force', 'Origin of Yorkist Charge', 'The Stanley Forces' and 'The Charge'.

As you proceed downhill you will pass through a wooden hand gate by the final sign, 'Henry Tudor's Front Line' and then go through a further gate where, by a 'Heart of the Battle' sign, a standard flies proudly. Cross the bed of the old Nuneaton railway station cutting (now restored as the Bosworth Light Railway). **Shenton station** and its car park lie ahead.

13 Rutland Water and Hambleton

A tranquil scene at Rutland Water

The Walk 4 miles 2½ hours
Map OS Explorer 234 Rutland Water (GR 900076)

How to get there

Hambleton can be found by turning off the A606 a mile east of Oakham.
Parking: Park with consideration by the church.

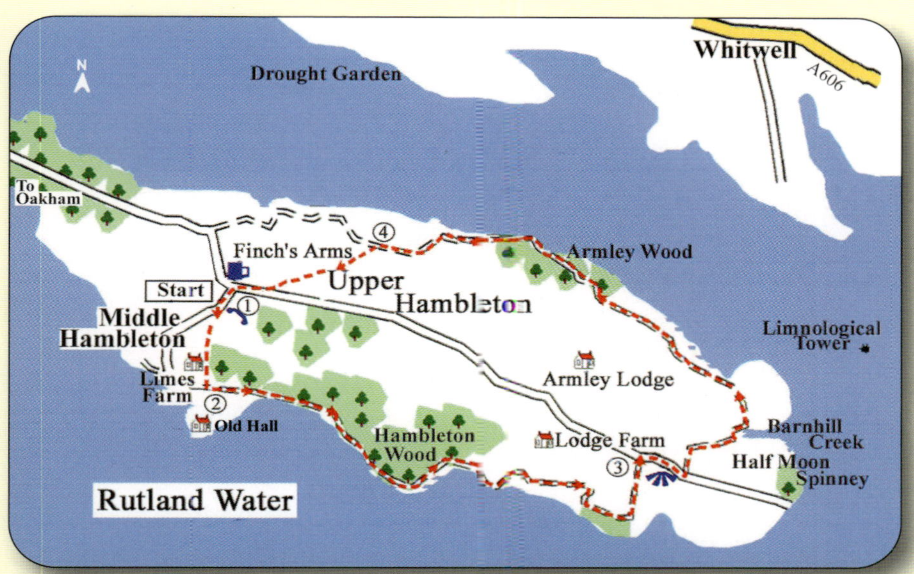

Introduction

The 'island' in the middle of Rutland Water is a rather special place and this is a wonderful walk to enjoy its special scenery. Hambleton is an historic and beautiful village situated on the Hambleton Peninsula, being surrounded on three sides by water. During this walk you will be able to enjoy a wonderful view across to Burley-on-the-Hill from the north side of the village; and to the south a sailing club can be seen on the far shore. In season the woods are full of bluebells.

Refreshments

The 17th-century **Finch's Arms** at Upper Hambleton is a traditional pub with low beams and with a delightful view over the water. Telephone: 01572 756575.

THE WALK

This area was, since before the Domesday Book, divided into three parts: Upper, Middle and Lower (or Nether) Hambleton, but in 1976 flooding of the lower land took place to create Rutland Water as a water source for Peterborough and its surrounding area. As a result Upper Hambleton and part of Middle Hambleton became known simply as 'Hambleton'. Nether Hambleton is now under Rutland Water, and excavation has shown it to have once been a sizeable medieval settlement. All that remains of Middle Hambleton are the Jacobean 'Old Hall', built in 1611 and now situated just at the water's edge, and some dwellings on the lower slope.

Sitting on top of the hill is the 12th-century church of St Andrew (originally probably the Saxon 'St Audrey'), with its low broach-spire and original Norman doorway. Restored elaborately in the 19th century, the church has fine stained-glass windows, mostly by J. Egan (1895-1900); the 16th-century 'Priest's House' may be seen below the church. Hambleton Hall, built in 1881 and now an hotel, used to be the Victorian home of Mrs Astley-Cooper, a friend of Noel Coward – who wrote Hay Fever *whilst a guest there. The 'estate cottages' of 1892 include the Hambleton Post and Telegraph Office (now closed), and an unusual art-nouveau clock.*

From the gates of beautiful **St Andrew's church** in Hambleton, proceed south down the lane towards the **Old Hall**. In about 150 yards veer left to walk a public footpath, proceeding over a stile to descend a field with a fine view of **Rutland Water** and the **Old Hall** immediately ahead. The view improves as you descend to go over a further stile onto a good track – the **Rutland Cycle Way**.

Turn left along the cycle way by the edge of **Rutland Water**. You are likely to see swans, ducks, coots and moorhens as you walk and the water is often dotted with fishing boats and the occasional sailing yacht. Proceed over the cattle grid and enter **Hambleton Wood**, which is managed by the Leicestershire and Rutland Wildlife Trust. Rabbit fencing protects the newly coppiced hazel and there is a nightingale breeding site. Here you can expect to hear birds chattering and there will be the occasional glimpse of the water through the trees to add to your pleasure. You will exit the wood over another cattle grid for a fine view over to the village of **Edith Weston** and an old museum on the bank opposite. Continue along the good easy track through **Hinman's Spinney** then veer northwards to reach a lane.

Turn right along the cycle way set to the right of the lane. Cross the lane and continue north/north-east by **Barnhill Creek** from where you will have a pleasing view across to **Whitwell** and the **Limnological Tower** which is set in the middle of Rutland Water.

St Andrew's church, Hambleton

The Limnological Tower is where the biological, chemical and physical characteristics of the stored water are monitored.

The track proceeds into **Armley Wood**, going over a cattle grid on entry and exit.

  ④

About 600 yards after leaving the wood, turn left over a stile and walk up by the right-hand hedge, going over a couple of stiles to reach a lane. Turn right and walk into **Upper Hambleton**, passing by some attractive thatched cottages, in particular **Dove Cottage** on the left. **Hambleton Post and Telegraph Office** is also a delightful old building near to the church, as you return to your car.

PLACE OF INTEREST NEARBY

Oakham, 3 miles west of the route, is the bustling county town of Rutland and is rich in history and character. Telephone Oakham Tourist Information Office on 01572 724329.

14 Wing, Lyndon and Rutland Water Nature Reserve

Lyndon's 4th-century church

The Walk 5 miles 🕐 3 hours
Map OS Explorer 234 Rutland Water (GR 895030)

How to get there

Wing lies to the east of the A6003 between Oakham and Uppingham. Turn off at Preston and follow the signs to Wing. **Parking:** In the lay-by on the main road in Wing.

Introduction

This easy walk takes you back in time through the most attractive Rutland village of Lyndon and on to Rutland Water Nature Reserve for fine views overlooking the famous reservoir. In Wing itself there is the chance to visit its rare turf maze.

Lyndon is set along a delightful lane lined with attractive Stamford stone houses. Local artists often take up position along the side of the lane to spend a peaceful day at their easel. Spare time to visit the beautiful St Martins of Tours church – built in AD 316 to AD 396 – which has a particularly fine and unusual rear archway. Lyndon is an estate village retaining much of its charm and rural character and providing an almost unique place to live. Today the estate extends to over 1,000 acres with the village at its centre.

Refreshments

The **Cuckoo Inn**, in the centre of Wing, is a traditional 17th-century pub. Telephone: 01572 737340.

THE WALK

From the main road in **Wing** proceed east to the road junction, signed to **Glaston**. To see the famous **maze**, turn right and it is situated less than 220 yards up the Glaston road.

Some 40 ft in diameter with grass banks about a foot high, there is some dispute as to the maze's original function although it is of a type seen in medieval times in other parts of England and in certain French cathedrals. History suggests that there was a monastery in Wing with a French connection around the 12th century. The design reflects those found on coins and medals from ancient Crete. Was this the maze of the Minotaur? It is

believed that religious penitents followed the maze on hands and knees, repeating prayers at certain points and finally reaching the centre. If true, the remarkable maze will have survived for some 800 years but there is an alternative opinion suggesting it was made by Gothic revivalists in the 18th century to romanticise a medieval myth.

From the maze, return to the main road, cross over and walk up the wide farm track opposite. The track descends gently north over the main-line railway via a couple of gates.

About 275 yards beyond the railway line you will cross a small bridge, a fine stone-built one over the **River Chater**. Bear right onto a further track that veers north-east

Wing's famous turf maze

along the side of a hedge.
Follow the clear waymarks, pausing
from time to time to enjoy a
pleasing retrospective view
of **Wing**.

 ③

The track becomes a footpath as it
enters trees and then passes by
Lyndon Hall to your left.

*Privately-owned Lyndon Hall is an
impressive building with a ha-ha in
front. Occupied by the Conant
family since 1670, the Hall holds a
special place in British scientific
history as the birthplace of Sir
Thomas Barker (1722-1809) who
carried out the most detailed study
of weather patterns of the time. His*

*meticulously-maintained record of
observations is still used by
meteorologists today.*

The clear path continues along the
back of attractive large gardens until
you reach a lane in the beautiful
village of **Lyndon**.

 ④

Go left along the lane into the
centre of the village. It is pleasant to
meander through this peaceful
village – like taking a step back in
time. Continue up the lane past the
Lodge entrance and in about 210
yards turn right through a gate into
pastureland, following the direction
of the fingerpost. Enter **Lyndon
Wood** through a gate.

Walk the clear path up through the wood and proceed up a hedged track to a gate onto the **Lyndon road**. Turn left along the road for about 210 yards to the road corner. Cross and head right, by the right-hand field hedge. After going through the corner gate, a fine view of **Rutland Water** unfolds and you will get a good view of **Upper Hambleton** and its **Old Hall** across the water. The path bears initially left then veers right, descending gently to reach a gate onto the **Rutland Cycle Way**. Turn left along the cycle way for about 550 yards to a lane by the visitor centre of the **Rutland Water Nature Reserve**. Created in 1970, the reserve attracts a wide variety of birds. Gadwall, shoveller, teal, tufted duck, pochard and shelduck are all present throughout the year. In spring one can see little gulls, arctic terns, black terns and the occasional rare Caspian or white-winged black tern. Among the summer visitors the common tern, the lapwing and the redshank may be seen. In winter the regular inmates are joined by pintail, goldeneye, goosander, wigeon and some other rarer ducks.

 ⑤

Head left and in about 375 yards, you reach the **Lyndon road** once again. Cross over the road and proceed ahead on the wide farm track to the right of a hedge. Walk this track, descending gently for the next mile until you arrive at the railway line. Cross over the railway line and ascend the wide and gentle farm track back to the main street in Wing. Spare time to take a look at its fine old stone buildings. The church is particularly interesting and the thatched **Cuckoo Inn** will welcome a thirsty walker.

15 Sibson, Sheepy Parva and Ratcliffe Culey

The fishing lake at Sheepy Parva

The Walk 5 miles 🕐 3 hours
Map OS Explorer 232 Nuneaton & Tamworth (GR 354008)

How to get there

Sibson is north-west of Hinckley and just off the A444. The walk starts by the Cock Inn. **Parking:** By the roadside in the village of Sibson.

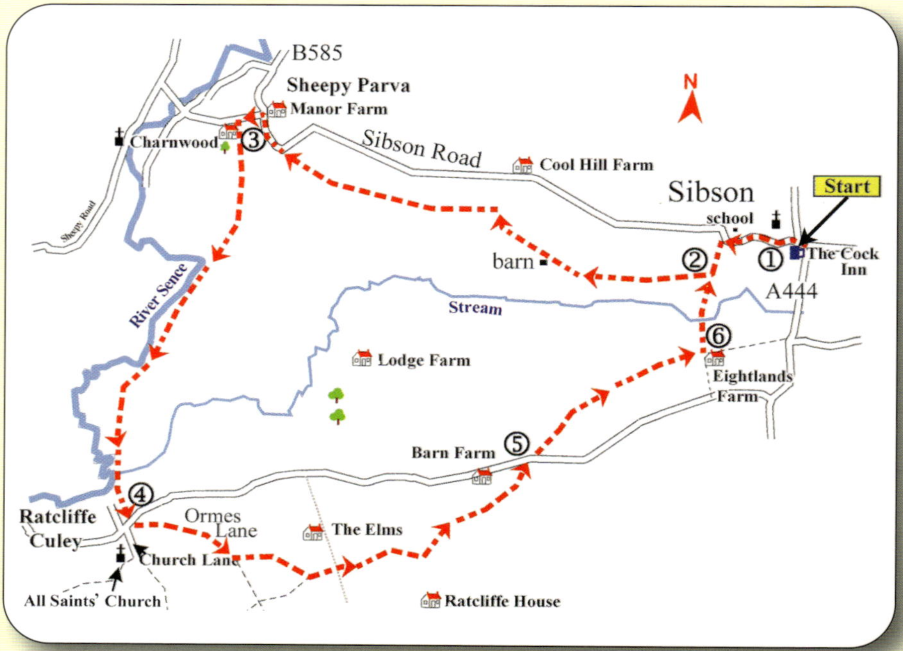

Introduction

This is a pleasing walk along a sleepy part of the Leicestershire Round. From Sibson, the first of three pretty villages, you head out along the bank of the attractive River Sence to Ratcliffe Culey, and then return through typically attractive Leicestershire farmland.

Refreshments

On your return to Sibson, the 13th-century **Cock Inn** is a beautiful thatched pub to complete a lovely day out. Telephone: 01827 880357.

THE WALK

① From the **Cock Inn**, walk into the village, passing by the interesting school house. At the road corner go left, following a waymarked path through a residential drive to the right of the corner house. Proceed on the narrow footpath, going over a stile into pastureland.

The thatched Cock Inn at Sibson

②

In about 150 yards, go right over a fence and proceed in a west/north-westerly direction over a series of fields and stiles. You pass by a Dutch barn and after about 1½ miles of easy walking you will go through a gate to arrive at a lane on the outskirts of **Sheepy Parva**.

③

Proceed into the village and go left onto the **Wellesbourne road** (the B585). In about 125 yards go left, to the left of a cottage called Charnwood. (If you can spare the time, walk further down the B585 pavement to admire a small attractive fishing lake.) The path goes generally south now until you are walking by the side of the pretty **River Sence**. Walk the path by the side of the stream over a series of fields and you are likely to see ducks and herons. As you approach the hamlet of **Ratcliffe Culey** you will go over a solid footbridge and ascend to the road. Go right and then left to walk up **Church Lane** to visit **All Saints' church**.

The name 'Ratcliffe Culey' dates back to feudal times when the estate was owned by the 'Culey' lords, one of whom was a famous philosophic writer. Ratcliffe is derived from 'Rede-clive' and probably refers to the division of some estate land by the lords of the manor. The population of Ratcliffe

Drive and Stroll

*has remained fairly constant –
although there were fewer dwelling
places in the past, families were
larger. The church registers go back
to 1585 and many of the
gravestones in the churchyard show
the names of old families, e.g. the
Wathes and the Eastons. Every
Whit Sunday a feast used to be
held for the villagers and on
St Thomas' Day the poor received
coals and the children bibles.*

Return back down **Church Lane** to
the main road and now go right
past the **Gate pub** to a junction of
roads. Here, go right and walk up
Ormes Lane. At the first corner, go
left (to the left of a house) along a
waymarked footpath which quickly
leads to cultivated farmland. Proceed
on this path over a series of fields
and stiles going generally in a
west/south-west direction, then
veering left to go over a farm track,
where the path bears north-west and
passes to the right of **Barn Farm**.

Cross the lane to continue in the
same general direction. In about
¾ mile you will reach a stile set to
the left of **Eightlands Farm**.

Go over the stile and proceed north
(left) over a footbridge to rejoin the
footpath which will lead you back
into the village of **Sibson**.

PLACE OF INTEREST NEARBY

Polesworth, 6 miles to the west, has a superb **abbey** that is worth a visit.
It was a Benedictine nunnery founded in the 9th century by St Modwena
and King Egbert. The first abbess was Edgytha, daughter of King Egbert,
now known as St Editha. Telephone Polesworth library for further
information: 01827 892587.

16 | Oadby

A shady path

The Walk 3 miles 2 to 3 hours
Map OS Explorer 233 Leicester & Hinckley (GR 651010)

How to get there

Oadby is situated some 3½ miles south of Leicester, on the A6.
Parking: Park with consideration in the entrance drive to the Karting Centre.

Drive and Stroll

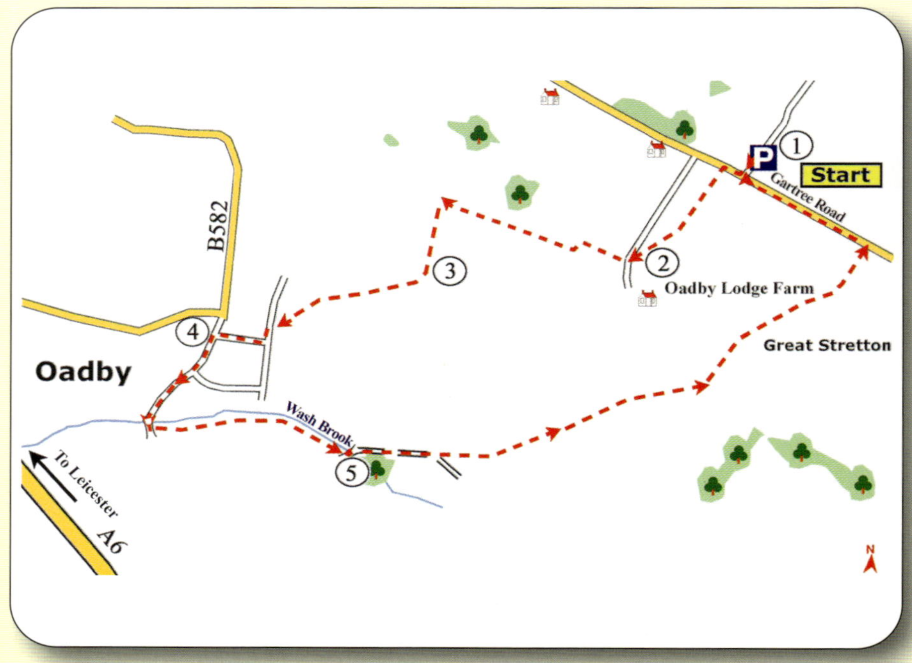

Introduction

This is an easy stroll around the park near Oadby, through trees and over open fields to the Wash Brook, and returning along more pleasant footpaths to the start.

The town became famous for its racecourse, which is situated on the border between Oadby and Leicester, and for the University of Leicester Botanic Garden. It is home to the Beauchamp College, and also has some halls of residence for the University of Leicester. In recent times the town is remembered by some, perhaps, because John Deacon, the bass player of the rock group Queen, was born and grew up in Oadby.

Refreshments

There are numerous places in Oadby including the **Lord Keeper of the Great Seal** in The Parade which is a Wetherspoon watering hole. Telephone: 01162 720957.

The **Fox Inn** in London Road is another good place for refreshment. Telephone: 01162 713102.

THE WALK

From the car proceed to **Gartree Road** and turn right. In about 50 yards cross over the busy road and go over the stile in the hedge opposite. Cross the farm field to a yellow waymark sign and proceed over a pair of stiles – you will see the buildings of **Oadby Lodge Farm** ahead and to your left. Diagonally cross the farm field to another stile.

Go over the stile and cross the entrance drive to **Oadby Lodge Farm** and continue along the clear footpath set to the left of trees. The route takes you around the edge of cultivated farm fields and soon you will veer right into the trees to continue along the footpath. In about 150 yards, turn left and walk down the clear stony footpath going generally southwards.

Turn right along the footpath towards **Oadby**. This will take you through a kissing gate and as you continue along the clear footpath you will arrive at another kissing gate on the edge of the town.

There has been a habitation here since AD 550. In 1760, on Brocks Hill, evidence of an Anglian burial ground was discovered. Oadby is one of 70 Danish settlements in Leicestershire ending with '-by', which means village or settlement. Danish rule continued until AD 920, when King Alfred the Great won his battles against the Danes. The Oadby area is supposed to be the site of at least one of these battles.

Proceed into the residential road called **Windrush Drive** and turn left. At the next road junction turn right and stroll to the end of a short residential road called **Tamar Road**.

Turn left into **Severn Road** and walk down this to cross over a bridge over **Wash Brook**. Turn left, along the clear footpath through the trees always with **Wash Brook** off to your left. Stroll along this pleasant footpath for about ½ mile.

Just after going through a hand gate, turn left, cross over **Wash Brook** via the wide timber bridge and bear right up the stone footpath. In about 150 yards the stone path goes right, through the hedge, but you continue ahead keeping to the left of the field hedge. Pass through the gap at the field end and continue along the clear footpath set to the left of the hedge, strolling in a generally north-easterly direction. Eventually you will reach a track coming in from

Wash Brook

your right. Bear left to join this track and proceed along this to **Gartree Road**. Turn left, cross over and turn right up the lane to the **Karting Centre** where you will find your parked car.

17 Lyddington and the Eyebrook Reservoir

The atmospheric Eyebrook reservoir

The Walk 5 miles 🕐 Allow 2 to 3 hours
Map OS Explorer 234 Rutland Water (GR 876970)

How to get there

Lyddington is situated just east of the A6003 between Uppingham and Corby and some 2 miles south of the A47. **Parking:** With consideration by the Green in Lyddington.

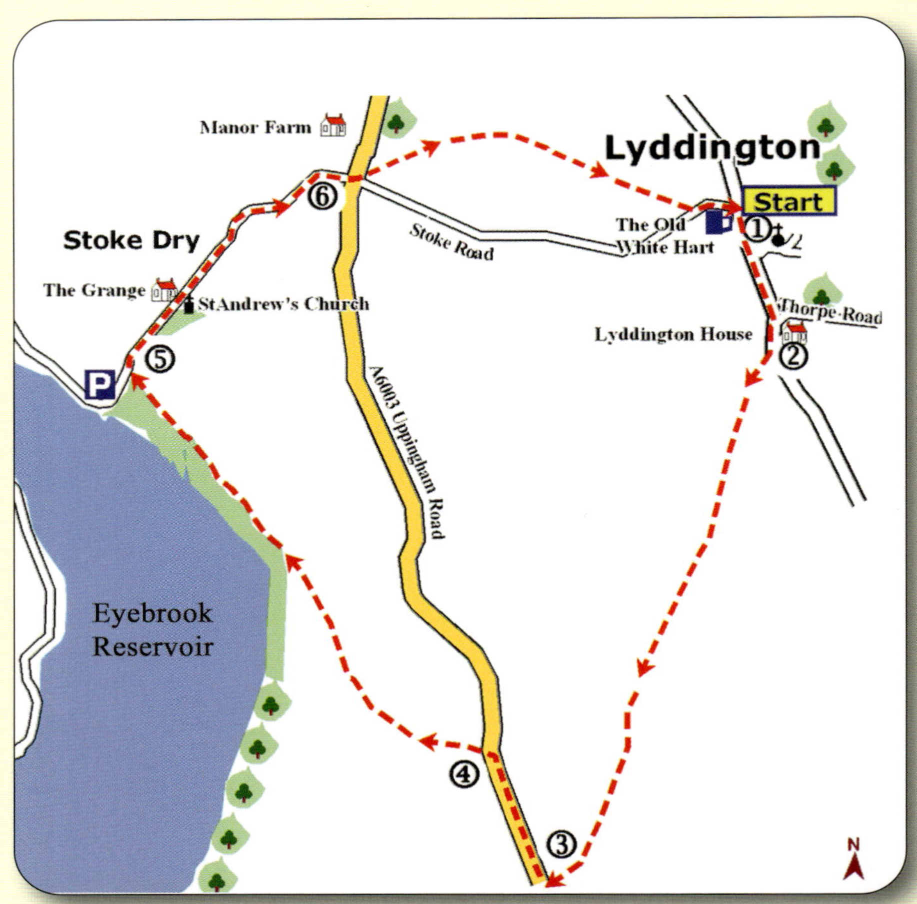

Introduction

This is a gentle stroll through the attractive villages of Lyddington and Stoke Dry, with a pleasing stretch near the beautiful Eyebrook Reservoir and a glimpse of the sites of two deserted medieval villages.

Refreshments

Both the **Old White Hart Inn** (telephone: 01572 821703) and the **Marquess of Exeter Hotel** in Lyddington (telephone: 01572 822477) are welcoming pubs offering a range of food.

THE WALK

In 1900, Rutlanders in other areas referred to the village as Long Lyddington and the villagers themselves were known as 'Lithers'. Although all the houses are now privately-owned, in the distant past, the Exeter Estate owned a large part of the village. The Bishop's Palace can be traced back to 1320; in 1490 it was properly rebuilt and in 1600 the Jesus Hospital in this building was founded by the Earl of Exeter as an asylum for needy persons. The Old Post Office at number 47 was run by the Cheadles for many years. It was a general store, selling men's clothes, boots and shoes. In the olden days, Stoke Road was called Pig Lane, relating to the time the pigs were penned on this road in readiness for the markets held in Lyddington.

From **the Green**, near the **Old White Hart**, head south down the main street, passing by the church, **Bede House** and **Thorpe Road** (on the left) and some fine old cottages on your right.

Shortly after passing **Lyddington House** on the left and near to the village hall, bear right following a clear footpath sign. You will go over a couple of stiles and through a small paddock to reach open pastureland and then pass by farm buildings on the left.

Initially keep by the hedge on the right and then veer south-west to diagonally cross a large field aiming for a waymarked stile in the far left corner – you will go over a small stream about halfway across the field. Go over the stile and proceed right, maintaining your south-westerly direction, diagonally crossing the next large field – you should find a clear path between the yellow-topped posts. Maintain your line over further stiles until you reach the A6003 near a silver piped works on the left.

Turn right along the grass verge of the A6003, taking time to observe some grassy humps and hollows on either side of the road. This is all that remains of the deserted medieval village of **Snelston**.

In about 500 yards, cross over the A6003 and go left through a hand gate, ascending a clear path to the top of the field. The path arcs right through a couple of hand gates and in front of you is a fine view overlooking **Eyebrook Reservoir** with the tower of **St Andrew's church** at **Stoke Dry** to its right.

Eyebrook Reservoir was formed by the damming of the Eye Brook and straddles the border between Leicestershire and Rutland. Built

during the 1930s by Stewarts and Lloyds, it was designed to supply water to their steel works at Corby – now part of Corus. During the Second World War the reservoir was used as a practice site for the dambuster raids. Since 1942 it has been a trout fishery and is now a Site of Special Scientific Interest.

Descend the clear path, enjoying the view as you walk towards a conifer spinney bordering the edge of the reservoir. Proceed through a series of farm gates along a wide, waymarked bridleway and you will eventually arrive at the **Stoke Dry Road**.

Turn right and ascend the road into the hamlet of **Stoke Dry**, pausing to visit the fascinating **St Andrew's church** on your right.

In the chantry chapel of St Andrew's are the Digby family paintings. One of the family members, Sir Everard Digby was involved in the Gunpowder Plot in 1605.

Continue to ascend the road past attractive houses and cottages, but pausing from time to time to capture the fine retrospective view over the reservoir. Where the road bends right you will pass the entrance to **Manor Farm** (on your left) and will soon arrive at the A6003 road once again.

 **6**

Cross over the A6003 and proceed over the stile to the left of the corner of **Stoke Road** opposite. Walk the clear waymarked path that initially runs parallel with a row of telegraph poles on your right. **Seaton Viaduct** should be visible to the right of the **Ketton Towers** and as you proceed through a gate the spire of **Lyddington church** will come into view. After going over several stiles you arrive back on the **Stoke Road**. Turn left and stroll along the quiet road into the village of **Lyddington**. At the road junction, go right back to the Green and the **Old White Hart Inn**.

On the way back to Lyddington

PLACE OF INTEREST NEARBY

Lyddington Bede House, originally part of the medieval bishops' palace, is now owned by English Heritage and open to the public. In 1860 it was the village school and in 1900 had a headmaster and three teachers. Visit www.english-heritage.org.uk or telephone: 01572 822438 for further information.

18 Burbage Common

At the start of the walk

The Walk 3½ miles 2½ hours
Map OS Explorer 233 Leicester & Hinckley (GR 447954)

How to get there

Burbage is situated to the south-west of Leicester and can be reached from junction 2 of the M69 or via the A47 from Leicester, north-west of Hinckley. **Parking:** In the free car park near the visitor centre on Burbage Common, off the B4668.

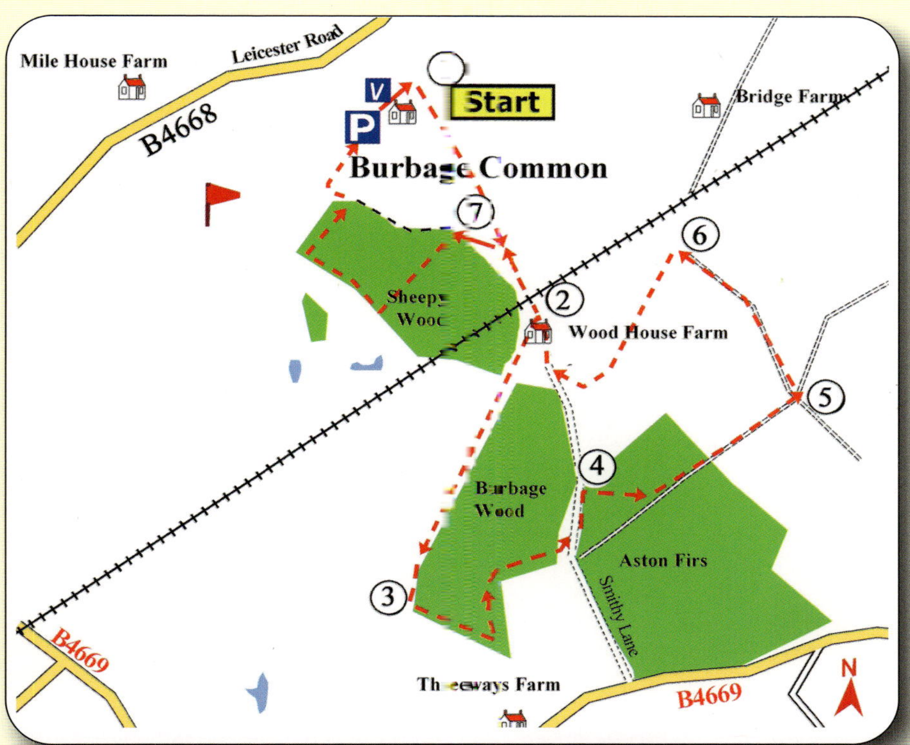

Introduction

This is a pleasing stroll around Burbage Common to visit a well established nature reserve. If you visit in April and May you will see masses of beautiful bluebells in the woods. Burbage Common comprises some 200 acres of semi-natural ancient woodland situated only about a mile from Hinckley. Here you can enjoy unspoilt grassland and should see many birds, fungi, wild flowers and invertebrates. There are picnic areas, permissive horse riding trails and several miles of public footpaths, and a visitor centre with displays about the common and the nature reserve.

Refreshments

The **Burbage Visitor Centre** offers light refreshments; telephone: 01455 633712. Otherwise in Hinckley itself you could visit the **Holy Well Inn** on London Road; telephone: 01455 234084.

THE WALK

From the car park take the footpath set to the left of the visitor centre until you reach and go under the railway line.

Bear right to continue along the clear footpath that will take you to a stile and the open countryside. You will be walking along pastureland outside **Burbage Wood** on a clear footpath. Ignore the footpaths that enter the wood in the first two fields as you pass over yet more stiles. Continue into the third field for about 100 yards.

Turn left into **Burbage Wood** and walk along the clear footpath inside the trees. This path goes around the outside edge of the wood and then arcs fairly sharply left, then right until you arrive on **Smithy Lane**. Turn left and stroll along the lane for about 100 yards.

Now, turn right into more woodland called **Aston Firs**. Walk along the clear footpath through the trees, going generally east. Later the path veers to the north-east and you will soon arrive back in open countryside and walk along a farm track set to the left of a field hedge.

At the field corner turn left and continue along a farm track sited to the left of the field hedge. Over the hedge to the right you will see the village of **Elmesthorpe** situated upon the hill (see Place of Interest). Eventually you will reach the end of the second field.

Turn left and stroll along a farm track set to the right of the field hedge. This is easy pleasant walking and soon you will be approaching **Burbage Common** with **Wood House Farm** set in the trees to the right ahead. At the end of the field you bear right and will exit the field to arrive back on the common via a new metal kissing gate. Turn right and pass beneath the railway bridge once again, retracing your steps back along the initial footpath for about 100 yards.

At a footpath sign turn left to leave the main footpath and you will soon see a signed entrance into **Sheepy Wood**. Walk the clear stony path through the wood, enjoying the beautiful bluebells in season, and soon you will arrive at its far end where you will see the golf course ahead through the trees. Now you turn right to continue along the footpath, with the golfers of Hinckley Golf Club to your left. At the end of the wood turn right once again and you will quickly arrive at an exit to the wood and bear left.

Ahead you will see the golf course once again but after about 50 yards you turn right and return back to the visitor centre on the common.

The nearby town of Hinckley has an ancient history going back to Saxon times. The name means the 'woodland clearing of a man called Hynca'. At the time of the Domesday Book, Hinckley had become a sizeable village, and grew over the course of the following 200 years into a small market town – a market being recorded there as long ago as 1311. Later, in the 17th century the town developed a hosiery industry. Hinckley played a prominent part in the English Civil War. Its proximity to several rival strongholds – including the Royalist garrisons at Ashby-de-la-Zouch and Leicester, meant that local townsfolk were forced to decide whether to declare their allegiances openly or to remain neutral. If they did not support the powers that operated at the time, they were forced to pay levies, ransoms, or fines to both sides. In March of 1644 the town was occupied by a group of Royalist troops who in turn were ousted by Parliamentarians, and townspeople were taken prisoner – a tough time for many.

A welcome seat in Sheepy Wood

PLACE OF INTEREST NEARBY

The small village of **Elmesthorpe** has strong connections with King Richard III and the Battle of Bosworth. It is said that the now partially ruined 13th-century church of St Mary provided shelter for the officers of Richard's army on their march from Leicester to the battle.

19 Foxton Locks

The Walk 3½ miles ⏱ 2 hours
Map OS Explorer 223 Northampton & Market Harborough
(GR 693892)

How to get there

Foxton is approximately 3 miles north-west of Market Harborough and can be accessed from the A6. **Parking:** The fee-paying car park at Foxton Locks.

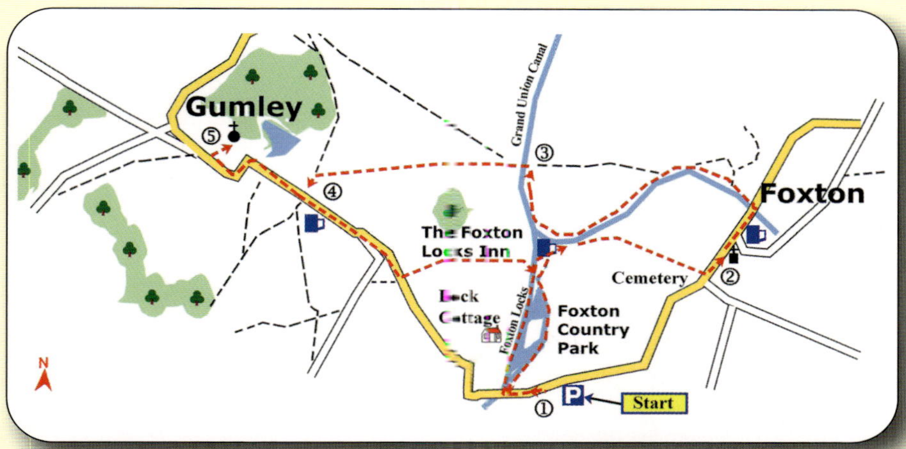

Introduction

This is a short meander by some of the finest canal locks in the UK but there is so much here that it makes a great day out for the whole family. From the locks, the route takes you into the nearby sleepy village of Gumley to see its fine church.

Refreshments

The **Foxton Locks Inn** is a picturesque pub by the canalside and offers food every day. Telephone: 01162 791515.

The **Bell Inn** at Gumley is an early 19th-century village pub with a cricket theme. There are bats and other memorabilia all over the place including a plate with David Gower's name on it. The pub is popular with local people serving a wide range of good value food.

THE WALK

 ①

Leave the car park and proceed to the top of the **Foxton flight** of lock gates, then descend to the towpath of the **Grand Union Canal** by the lock gates.

The Grand Union is a rather special canal and at Foxton you will enjoy seeing the series of ten locks called the Foxton Staircase. It is a tourist attraction and very popular, particularly during the summer. The locks, a remarkable feat of engineering which made the canal the M25 of its day, produced a spectacular rise of 75 ft from Market Harborough, some 20 miles from the summit. At the top, you will see the original two lock houses while at the bottom of the Staircase there is another lock house, plus the former canal company offices, a carpenter's shop, smithy and stabling, all converted for pleasure boat facilities.

The canal is a spawning site for the common toad, while the fish to look out for include pike, bream and chub. Near the banks, grass snakes are not uncommon, and birds such as the sedge warbler can often be found nesting.

You will pass near to the inclined plane, which you may wish to visit now, or on your return.

Just after passing the bottom lock, head right over the bridge past the small café, shop and pub, aiming towards the village of **Foxton**.

 ②

Head left along the road passing the church and the village pub and once over the canal bridge, turn left and descend to the towpath, keeping the canal on your left. After passing under **bridge 62**, follow the arm of the canal to a small brick and iron pedestrian bridge and cross over this.

 ③

Turn left and then proceed ahead along the side of a field hedge, going away from the canal. At the field end go over the fence-stile and proceed ahead over the next field to a gate set to the left of a sewage plant. Continue along the now enclosed footpath and ascend the hill to reach the road into **Gumley**.

'A horse and lad' adorn the towpath

The popular Foxton Locks Inn

Gumley is a small, sleepy village with no noisy shops and no street lights. It is an old village of considerable antiquity and is said to hide many mysteries. In the 8th century the village was called Godmundesleah – the 'lea' or woodland clearing of a man called Godmund. Godmund, according to some Early English scholars, could be read as 'Good Guardian', leading some local historians to make remarkable claims about the village – is there really an association with King Arthur? The village is located above a ridge, and the natural terrain would have produced a form of fortification – there is evidence of a defensive ditch on the boundary of the village, which local people have often referred to, colloquially, as 'Offa's Dyke'. Gumley's more recent past was dominated by Gumley Hall, which was built in 1764 by Joseph Craddock. The parish church of St Helen is one of the most picturesque churches in Leicestershire as it nestles within the grounds of the old hall.

 ④

Turn right and stroll into and through this quiet village, to its beautiful church.

 ⑤

Retrace your steps along the road past the old butcher's shop and the village pub. Bear left at the T-junction and in about another 200 yards turn left again through a gateway. Keep the hedge on your left and go through the gate at the end of the field to reach the canal bridge at the bottom of **Foxton Locks**. Turn right and retrace your steps back to the car park.

20 Peatling Parva and surrounding villages

Peatling Hall seen from the parkland

The Walk 5 miles ⏱ 3 hours
Map OS Explorer 233 Leicester & Hinckley (GR 589897)

How to get there

Peatling Parva is just south of Leicester and can be accessed from the A426 Leicester to Rugby road. **Parking:** By the roadside in Peatling Parva.

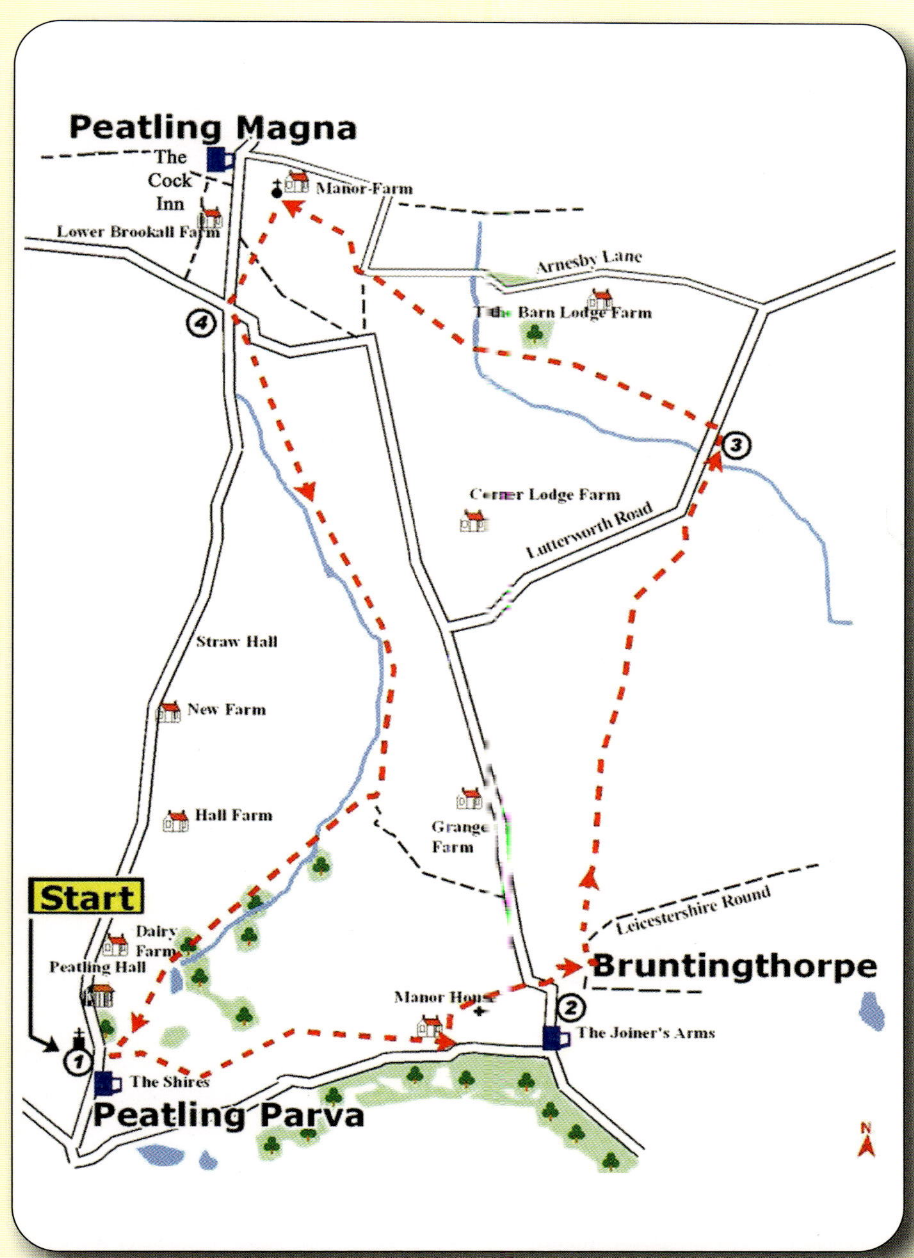

Peatling Magna
The Cock Inn
Manor Farm
Lower Brookall Farm
4
Arnesby Lane
The Barn Lodge Farm
3
Corner Lodge Farm
Lutterworth Road
Straw Hall
New Farm
Hall Farm
Start
Dairy Farm
Peatling Hall
Grange Farm
Leicestershire Round
Bruntingthorpe
Manor House
2
The Joiner's Arms
1
The Shires
Peatling Parva
N

93

Introduction

This is an easy walk in attractive Leicestershire countryside, walking by a pleasant stream. You will pass through several attractive villages and walk close to the impressive building of Peatling Hall.

Refreshments

The **Cock Inn** in Peatling Magna is a welcoming country pub. Telephone: 01162 478308. There is also the **Joiner's Arms** at Bruntingthorpe. Telephone: 01162 478258.

THE WALK

From the road in **Peatling Parva**, proceed down the enclosed path set to the left of the thatched white house to reach the open countryside and follow the sign to **Bruntingthorpe**. Proceed down the field going over a field corner stile and a footbridge to pass through young plantations and cross over a stream via a plank bridge. Ascend the next field, go over the stile by a field gate and proceed to the far right corner of the next field. Now turn right and walk the field edge of the next field to another stile. Go over this and head left through a farm gate by a tall corrugated iron shed and some farm sheds going over yet another stile to reach the drive way entrance to **Manor House Farm** in **Bruntingthorpe**.

Go right and walk to the road. Bear left over a stile passing to the left of the beautiful small church. Exit the churchyard via a kissing gate and carry on along **Church Walk** into the centre of the village – you will pass near the **Joiner's Arms** and a superb thatched house. Continue down to the main road and turn right past the corner garage.

At the next road corner, go left and walk **Little End** past some very attractive houses. At the end of the lane bear left passing a house called **Staplecourt**.

Turn left and go over a stile to continue in a northward direction, maintaining this walk line over the next seven fields and waymarked stiles – the small stream will be on your left. Where the stream bends across the path, bear right over the stile and aim for a big ash tree in the far right corner of the second field. Diagonally cross the next field and, as you go over the hedge, aim to the left of the red-brick building crossing a foot-plank to reach the **Lutterworth road**.

Turn right and walk the road towards **Arnesby**.

The pub at Bruntingthorpe

③

At the footpath signs, turn left over a stile passing by a large barn. Maintain your walk line over the next two fields aiming for a midfield waymark sign. At the sign bear right aiming towards the spire of **Peatling Magna church** ahead, diagonally crossing the large field and continuing until you reach a final stile at the bottom of the field below **All Saints' church**. Ascend the field and go through the churchyard and here turn left and stroll through the churchyard exiting via a hand gate at its rear. Now bear right, crossing pastureland and walking a sunken way to arrive in a field. Maintain your walking line over this field and go over the stile onto the **Peatling Parva road** by a road junction.

④

At the junction turn left and go over a field corner stile – you are now walking the waymarked **Leicestershire Round**. Follow the waymarker direction and you will cross over a cart bridge and go over a series of stiles with a stream to your right. At the beginning of the fourth field there is an old telephone exchange building at the top of the field. Continue over a further stile walking close to the stream as you progress over the next 3 fields.

As you approach the end of the third field you leave the **Leicestershire Round** and go right to reach a spinney. Proceed to the right of the spinney and at the stile, turn left and walk by the side of the field fence – the stream still to your right. At the field end bear right and go over a cart bridge over the stream (near to an old brick barn).

Soon you will be walking through a small plantation to arrive in the parkland of **Peatling Hall** passing in front of the impressive hall with its small ornate lake and attractive waterfalls – llamas may greet you in the park grounds. Aim for the large conifer in the far right-hand field corner and you will pass by two lovely white dwellings – one very finely thatched – and you will see **St Andrew's church**. If you have time, why not meander around the small attractive village where you will find the **Shires pub** if you are in need of refreshment.

PLACE OF INTEREST NEARBY

Stanford Hall, 5 miles to the south, has been the home of the Cave family since 1430. The River Avon flows gently through its park and the beautiful hall is open to the public on select days throughout the year. Telephone: 01788 860250; www.stanfordhall.co.uk